SOCIAL MEDIA IN THE FASHION INDUSTRY

This book introduces social network fundamentals in the fashion domain. It addresses the creation of social media marketing plans, highlighting strategic approaches that allow fashion brands to differentiate themselves in the ephemeral and challenging fashion context.

Through a variety of academic and professional sources and by sharing the results of their own research, the authors present research methodologies, including netnography, visual, sentiment and argumentation analysis, for developing rigorous studies to gain social media insights that can be useful for decision-making and value creation. The book also discusses future trends regarding social media management in the fashion domain via interviews with senior fashion experts.

This cutting-edge book that combines theory and practice will appeal to undergraduate and master students across a broad range of fields including fashion studies, marketing, digital marketing and communication and to young professionals who are starting to work in social media. In addition, this book is also developed for young researchers and PhD students employing social media analysis in their studies.

Patricia SanMiguel is Associate Professor of Digital Marketing, Influence Marketing and Fashion Consumer Behavior at the School of Communication at the University of Navarra (Pamplona, Spain), and ISEM Fashion Business School (Madrid, Spain).

Tekila Harley Nobile is Lecturer and Researcher in Luxury Business at Sotheby's Institute of Art (London, UK). She is Visiting Lecturer in Digital Fashion Communication at USI—Università della Svizzera italiana, Lugano (Switzerland).

Cristina Sánchez-Blanco is Professor at the School of Communication in the University of Navarra, Spain.

Nadzeya Sabatini is Assistant Professor in Digital Transformation at Gdansk University of Technology (Gdansk, Poland) and Senior Researcher at USI-Universita' della Svizzera Italiana (Lugano, Switzerland).

Routledge Studies in the Fashion Industry

This series explores the fashion industry through an interdisciplinary lense, bringing together cutting-edge research to define and advance this growing field. We welcome proposals for original research projects that are either single or multi-authored or an edited collection from both established and emerging scholars across the globe, working across the fashion industry. Topics include, but are not limited to, marketing, retailing, brand management, sustainability and supply chain management.

1. **Marketing Fashion**
   Critical Perspectives on the Power of Fashion in Contemporary Culture
   Edited by Karin M. Ekström

2. **Social Media in the Fashion Industry**
   Fundamentals, Strategy and Research Methods
   Patricia SanMiguel, Tekila Harley Nobile, Cristina Sánchez-Blanco and Nadzeya Sabatini

For a full list of titles in this series, please visit https://www.routledge.com

SOCIAL MEDIA IN THE FASHION INDUSTRY

Fundamentals, Strategy and Research Methods

Patricia SanMiguel, Tekila Harley Nobile, Cristina Sánchez-Blanco and Nadzeya Sabatini

Routledge
Taylor & Francis Group
LONDON AND NEW YORK

Designed cover image: onurdongel © Getty Images

First published 2024
by Routledge
4 Park Square, Milton Park, Abingdon, Oxon OX14 4RN

and by Routledge
605 Third Avenue, New York, NY 10158

Routledge is an imprint of the Taylor & Francis Group, an informa business

British Library Cataloguing-in-Publication Data
A catalogue record for this book is available from the British Library

ISBN: 978-1-032-82656-1 (hbk)
ISBN: 978-1-032-82657-8 (pbk)
ISBN: 978-1-003-50549-5 (ebk)

DOI: 10.4324/9781003505495

Typeset in Times New Roman
by Apex CoVantage, LLC

CONTENTS

FIGURES AND TABLES

Figures

Tables

ABOUT THE AUTHORS

Patricia SanMiguel

Patricia is Associate Professor of Digital Marketing, Influence Marketing and Fashion Consumer Behavior at the School of Communication at the University of Navarra and ISEM Fashion Business School. Patricia SanMiguel holds an Advertising and Public Relations Bachelor's Degree at Complutense of Madrid University (2011) and a PhD in Applied Creativity at the University of Navarra (Extraordinary PhD Award, 2018). She also holds an Executive Fashion MBA at ISEM. San Miguel is Visiting Scholar at USI—Università della Svizzera italiana and Università Cattolica del Sacro Cuore and Visiting Researcher at the Fashion Institute of Technology in New York and the University of Florence's Department of Economics and Management. San Miguel has been Principal Researcher in two European projects regarding Social Media and Influencer Marketing funded by the European Commission. In addition, she collaborates as a digital marketing advisor for fashion brands and entrepreneurs.

Tekila Harley Nobile

Tekila Harley Nobile is Lecturer and Researcher in Luxury Business at Sotheby's Institute of Art (London, UK). She is Visiting Lecturer in Digital Fashion Communication at USI—Università della Svizzera italiana (Switzerland). Her knowledge areas include strategic marketing, customer relationship management and customer experience, with a focus on the fashion and luxury sectors. Tekila holds a PhD awarded by the Institute of Digital Technologies for Communication, USI—Università della Svizzera italiana; an MA in Strategic Fashion Marketing from London College of Fashion; and a BSc in International Marketing from the University of Southampton and The Chinese University of Hong Kong.

Cristina Sánchez-Blanco

Cristina Sánchez-Blanco, PhD, is Professor at the School of Communication of the University of Navarra (Pamplona, Spain). Her research interest covers account planning, strategic planning, branding and advertising, digital marketing strategy and the financing sources of digital native media, in particular advertising, branded content and e-commerce. She is Visiting Scholar at The University of North Carolina at Chapel Hill, Chapel Hill, North Carolina, the United States, and Visiting Researcher at the Hartman Center for Sales, Advertising and Marketing History at Duke University, Durham, North Carolina, the United States. She is Head of the Marketing and Media Management Department at the University of Navarra.

Nadzeya Sabatini

Nadzeya Sabatini holds a PhD in Communication Sciences. She is Assistant Professor in Digital Transformation at Gdansk University of Technology (Gdansk, Poland). Nadzeya is Senior Lecturer and Academic Coordinator of MSc in Digital Fashion Communication, a double degree from USI—Università della Svizzera italiana (Lugano, Switzerland) and Universite' Paris 1 Pantheon-Sorbonne (Paris, France). She is Group Leader in Digital Fashion Communication Research at the Institute of Digital Technologies for Communication (USI). Nadzeya's research interests are in the digital transformation of communication in fashion and luxury domains. Nadzeya has been Visiting Researcher in Hong Kong, the UK, New Zealand and Portugal thanks to the excellence research scholarships of the Swiss National Science Foundation.

ACKNOWLEDGEMENTS

The authors would like to express their gratitude to colleagues who provided guidance, feedback and in-depth knowledge on their area of expertise.

A special thank-you to Professor Sara Greco and Chiara Mercuri for their insights on argumentation analysis; Professor Katharina Lobinger, Dr Rebecca Venema and Dr Seraina Tarnutzer for their guidance on visual analysis; and Professor Ulrike Gretzel for her advice on netnography analysis.

INTRODUCTION

Fashion and communication are highly interconnected. Fashion is communication, it is the channel through which people express themselves, their identity and their personality.

The overlapping areas of fashion and information communication technologies (ICTs) are crucial as fashion brands increasingly adopt communication technologies to reach consumers and develop relationships with them.

Today, social media is a widely adopted channel by fashion brands to communicate with consumers. Social media is one of the most recent and fastest-developing domains that have considerably impacted the traditional communication strategies of fashion brands. Through social networks, millions of people stay in contact with each other and brands, while sharing information and maintaining personal and professional relationships. Fashion and social media are a perfect match as they rely on text and images to communicate. They can be both personal and professional, individual/local and global.

Every year, more and more people adopt social networks, spend more time on them and develop and maintain social relationships on digital platforms. Hence, fashion companies want to be present on these digital platforms to be close to their customers at all times.

The fashion industry is constantly evolving, impacting, on the one hand, the way in which brands communicate and, on the other hand, the way in which customers consume. Arguably, such evolution is partly due to the transformation of communication channels, such as that of social networks, which is the focus of this book. For example, events such as fashion shows have been traditionally associated with the elite. However, thanks to social networks and their features, anyone today can potentially enjoy a fashion show.

DOI: 10.4324/9781003505495-1

The fashion industry has found social networks to be the perfect ally to interact with consumers. Social networks, initially adopted as a channel to communicate the brand's story and its products to attract new consumers and generate brand awareness, are now also utilised to develop two-way communication with consumers, share entertaining content and facilitate users' day-to-day lives. In this way, social networks have become a channel to amplify marketing strategies, develop advertising campaigns and generate value through brand loyalty. Thus, many social media profiles have become customer service channels and even sales platforms, thanks to real-time user interaction.

Recognising the potential of social networks, fashion brands are focusing on developing professional and mature social media marketing strategies to create personal relationships with existing and potential users, clients and the community.

This book critically defines the concept of social media communication within the complex fashion communication ecosystem. It presents in a dynamic way the fundamentals of social media marketing for fashion companies, its power and potential risks by relying on a vast range of academic and professional sources.

This book aims to provide a background understanding of social media networks that will last over time beyond specific platforms while considering the implications for the fashion industry.

This book has four main objectives:

1. Introduce the fundamentals of social networks in the fashion domain
2. Explain how to create a social media marketing plan, highlighting a strategic approach that enables brands to be differentiated from the competition while considering the ephemeral and challenging fashion context
3. Offer relevant academic and professional research tools and methodologies for developing rigorous studies to gain social media insights useful for decision-making, strategy development and value creation
4. Present the point of view of selected fashion brands through in-depth interviews on their social media strategies and trends

This book is primarily conceived for fashion, marketing and communication undergraduate and master students and young professionals who are beginning in social media. In addition, this book is developed for all those young researchers and fashion industry professionals who wish to conduct in-depth social media academic studies in the fashion communication field.

The book is structured in five sections.

The first section, *Fashion Social Media Fundamentals,* comprises two chapters. Chapter 1 describes the power of social media and its impacts on fashion companies. It focuses on three characteristics of social media: interaction, engagement and communication. Chapter 2 explains how individuals build their identities through social networks and how they behave on these platforms. Finally, it explains the segmentation of marketing campaigns and the importance of identifying and understanding fashion consumer behaviour.

The second section, *Social Media Strategy and Plan*, consists of two chapters. Chapter 3 explains how to design a social media strategy, including performing the social media audit and competitor analysis, defining objectives and target audience and designing the campaign's message. Chapter 4 introduces the main characteristics of social networks that fashion companies can adopt to develop their plans.

The third section, *Social Media Performance*, consists of four chapters. This section explains how to create a social media commerce strategy by creating a content plan. It introduces the steps that should be followed to create a strong community and CRM strategy, and it describes how to manage a social media calendar. Subsequently, it presents insights regarding budgeting and the importance of monitoring the social media plan through management tools.

The fourth section, *Social Media Research Opportunities and Methodologies*, introduces the opportunities and challenges of conducting social media research. It comprises four chapters, presenting four social media research methodologies that can support brands in evaluating their performance on social media channels or can be used in fashion-communication-related research projects. The methodologies presented are netnography, sentiment, visual and argumentation analysis.

Finally, the fifth section, *Interviews with Fashion Brands*, presents a set of conversations with selected senior professionals from fashion companies to provide examples of how they approach and manage their social media profiles, the main difficulties they encounter and possible developments they foresee.

SECTION 1

Fashion Social Media Fundamentals

This first part of the book introduces the reader to the basics of social media from a fashion industry perspective. In this book, 'fundamentals' refer to those notions that are key to developing a successful social media strategy.

Communication and marketing professionals must have an in-depth knowledge of their digital platforms and users interested in their brands and products. Such knowledge is crucial to offer users an enriching digital experience, products that fit their needs and wants and content in which they are interested and build lasting relationships. Social networks can offer in-depth knowledge regarding individuals and their digital identity, their personalities, the impact of social networks on their lives and how they behave and interact on these platforms, representing the great potential for fashion brands.

This section consists of two chapters.

- Chapter 1, ***The Power of Social Media***, presents three key elements of social media and their impact on the fashion domain: interaction, engagement and communication.
- Chapter 2, ***Fashion Consumer and Social Media***, focuses on digital social identity and social media behaviour. It stresses the importance of understanding social networks' impacts on users as it is essential to develop consumer-focused plans. In addition, it explains the potential of segmentation to develop personalised social media network plans.

DOI: 10.4324/9781003505495-2

After reading this section, you will:

- Grasp how social networks impact society
- Understand how social media networks help brands interact, engage and communicate with consumers
- Evaluate the concept of digital social identity, how it develops on social networks and its relationship with the fashion industry
- Gain insights on how knowledge regarding users' digital behaviour can be utilised to create effective and personalised social media strategies
- Understand segmentation practices on social media
- Learn how to interpret user-generated content and analytics

1

THE POWER OF SOCIAL MEDIA

Introduction

'Social media are the online means of communication, conveyance, collaboration, and cultivation among interconnected and interdependent networks of people, communities, and organisations enhanced by technological capabilities and mobility' (Tuten and Solomon, 2018, p. 28). Consumers no longer see brands only as brands as they do not expect just products and services from them; they look for interaction, engagement and communication, three aspects central to social media. We will describe these concepts in the next sections.

Interaction

Consumers are no longer passive recipients of brands' communication. Instead, they can actively participate and engage on social media.

On the one hand, social networks represent useful spaces for those consumers who want to participate in the brand's decision-making process (Thomas et al., 2020). On the other hand, we no longer talk only about user-generated content or influencer content (SanMiguel, 2020) but also about *content creation,* which brings value to brands and consumers, respectively. The current circumstances, technological development and the possibility for creators to monetise their content make it a more interesting reality. Most social networks are introducing features to enable users to monetise their work. 'By using creators to tap into these circles where you are not well known and adding value there, you will reach new audiences, build cultural relevance, and learn more about your customers' (Hootsuite, 2022, p. 12).

DOI: 10.4324/9781003505495-3

We can differentiate the influencer from the content creator. Following Scaman in the WARC guide (2021, p. 14) titled 'Creator Economy':

> One grows a social following through an artfully curated life, turning themselves into a palatable canvas in order to attract the attention of relevant brands, who can easily slot into their world of considered, edited, and polished perfection. The other leans into their talents or a specific topic, creating content that's entertaining, educational or engaging enough to grow a strong and sticky community, which they, in turn, can leverage in numerous ways to turn their followers into their financiers—through tiered access, merch lines, product spin-offs, virtual drops and much more. Put simply, one monetises their audience through brands, and the other monetises their audience directly.

In fact, TikTok developed the Creator Fund, which 'rewards creators for doing what they do best—making incredible TikTok videos. It's TikTok's way of celebrating and supporting creators for their dedication, ingenuity, and spirit.' (TikTok, 2022). By working with content creators, brands add new value to customers, reach new audiences, build cultural relevance and learn more about their customers (Hootsuite, 2022, p. 12).

In particular, some beauty brands are migrating to their community platforms and 'shifting focus from the major social media channels to new beta platforms such as Newness and Supergreat' (WARC, 2021, p. 25). 'The creator economy is driven by passionate individuals who share their interests with an engaged community and generate income from their knowledge and skills,' and the power of the creator economy is based on the ability of these creators to cater content to a special interest or a specific niche and 'community commerce will provide a space where creators and brands can build the high levels of engagement that drive inspiration and purchase' (WARC, 2022, p. 33).

Inspiration and purchase are two of the most relevant keywords when discussing interaction on social media. These have become even more relevant with livestream commerce (Liu and Cantoni, 2023; Lu and Chen, 2021; Wongkitrungrueng et al., 2020). Regarding social commerce, it can be said that 'social becomes the heart of modern shopping' (Hootsuite, 2022, p. 29). Social media has become one of the top sources of information about brands, second only to search engines. For 16- to 24-year-olds, it is the first source of information (Hootsuite and We are Social Digital, 2022).

Moreover, social media networks create a favourable environment for consumers to have different shopping experiences. Most importantly, consumers are using social media in all phases of the purchase journey: To get information, get inspired, do research, evaluate brands, purchase and share their experiences (Bhalla, 2014; Lynch and Barnes, 2020; Portela et al., 2021). It is understood by the constant need of human beings to seek needed information that is easier to be provided by the brands through social networks (Roberts and David, 2020).

Fashion brands understand well the role and value of social media for a fashion brand's success. Nike, for instance, uses its:

> SNKRS and Run Club apps to foster in-person meet-ups, running groups, and events. Its Training Club app delivers individual workouts and multi-week fitness programs. These investments allow Nike to create experiences that go far beyond their shoe and apparel lines and fold the brand into an individual's day-to day-routines.
>
> *(McKinsey, 2021)*

Engagement

We have previously discussed the benefits of interaction and working with content creators to nurture strong communities with valuable content. Since its origin, social media has sought to generate, expand and strengthen communities (Ananda et al., 2019). Indeed, 'social media are first and foremost about community: the collective participation of members who together create value' (Tuten and Solomon, 2018, p. 132).

As participation in online communities and social networks continues to become popular for fashion (De Valck et al., 2009), the relevance of understanding the impacts on consumer behaviour has also grown (Castillo-Abdul et al., 2022; Kaplan and Haenlein, 2010; Scaraboto and Fischer, 2013). 'Online communities are based upon new technologies' ability to facilitate a platform where consumers can carry out behaviours of sharing and gaining' (Nash, 2019, p. 85). Hence, brands can use social media to promote and nurture these communities.

Consumers are looking up to social media for entertaining experiences that combine content, commerce and gaming. The metaverse is gaining momentum, making experiences more immersive and connecting offline and online realities (Berger et al., 2018). 'Gaming is increasingly becoming an extension of the real world, and with the pandemic supercharging participation, it has become a prime target for fashion brands. Ralph Lauren, for instance, partnered with South Korean social network app ZEPETO to create a virtual fashion collection where users could dress their avatars in exclusive products or appearance-altering "skins" (McKinsey and The Business of Fashion, 2022, p. 58). Such connections between the fashion and gaming worlds are highly supported by the affordances of social media platforms (Noris et al., 2023).

The report called 'The Metaverse Explained' (Deloitte, 2022) discussed how immersive and interactive the Metaverse is, with a community aspect at the core. It can also include user-generated content and ownership. Besides, it states how gaming companies, social media companies and entertainment companies are already collaborating in this space. For instance, this can be seen in the outputs of the Metaverse Fashion Week initiative, which took place on March 24, 2022.

Communication

Consumers are looking for personal communication with brands. They demand brands to be transparent, authentic and trustworthy. In this way, social networks have become the right place for brands to achieve this close relationship with consumers.

On the one hand, social media networks have always been the perfect platforms for customer care; for example Twitter has been characterised by immediate, convenient and effective service (Misopoulus et al., 2014). On the other hand, faced with the demand for authenticity and social responsibility, social listening and social intelligence have become essential in the fight against misinformation (Hubspot, 2022). Fake news and misinformation, disseminated for economic, ideological or other reasons (Salaverría and León, 2022), find their perfect divulgation on social media. Yet, a major effort is invested in fighting misinformation on social media platforms, and important work is still to be done.

In addition, consumers' desires for personalised content (Nobile and Cantoni, 2022, 2023) lead to the development of niche social media platforms for a homogeneous group of consumers who can be offered the added value of exclusive content tailored to their interests and needs. 'The fundamental premise of these niche community platforms is to provide passionate individuals access to content that will truly speak to them and connect them with similar enthusiasts' (Vaughan, 2020).

Another interesting aspect related to these ideas is how brand advertising on social media is increasingly tied to the particularities of the network itself (Voorveld et al., 2018). The platforms, in fact, encourage brands to make their content fit organically into the platforms. We can take the examples of the following calls for action from social media networks such as 'Don't make ads. Make TikToks,' Pinterest's 'Stop interrupting, start inspiring' or 'Become a part of Snapchatters' everyday conversations.'

In conclusion, as we have seen while deep diving into social media management, it is necessary to start with an introduction to general aspects of social media, understanding how the digital identity is constructed, how segmentation is done and how consumer trends fit seamlessly with the performance and evolution of the social media platforms themselves.

Understanding the possibilities brands have to relate and connect with consumers through social networks is an essential starting point for understanding how fashion brands should approach their social media strategy and plan.

Implications of Social Media for Fashion Brands

The implementation of adequate social media strategies creates new competitive advantages and facilitates communication and marketing strategies in a global business environment (Kalbaska, et al, 2018; Kontu and Vecchi, 2014). In this way, we can discuss five key principles that highlight the relevance of carrying out adequate social media marketing strategies for/by fashion companies (García-San Miguel, 2017; Ferrándiz et al., 2016):

- Communities and advocacy. Through the information shared by users, fashion companies can obtain information about their brand image; opinions related to new collections, product and service satisfaction levels and users' preferences, desires, feelings and attitudes. This information can be used to learn how to redesign collections, flagship stores or online sales tools.
- Personalisation and exclusivity. Brands can identify their audience preferences and need to generate close relationships and personalise their marketing actions and strategies. Through social networks, brands can offer special discounts, invite their followers to events or broadcast live.
- Innovation. Social networks can help in the development of new products, the design of new processes or the evolution of business models. Social media platforms are actively adding new utilities, more powerful analysis tools or technological innovations day after day. Fashion brands can use active social media consumers as prosumers to test or launch new products. The result of such tests can lead to the redesign of garments or accessories before they are mass-marketed or even produced.
- Advertising and marketing. We must not forget that social media platforms generate their income through advertising. What they sell to advertisers is the possibility of reaching large audiences but with a high level of personalization. They can do this by obtaining and managing user data. Otherwise, as it is already happening, some social media networks will evolve into e-commerce platforms that can ultimately retain a large part of the product margin.
- All/new business models. Social networks can enable the creation and dissemination of disruptive schemes. Small start-ups with a good understanding of the exponential resonance mechanisms in social networks can quickly generate new business models adapted to the real needs or preferences of consumers.

Bibliography

Ananda, A.S., Hernández-García, Á., Acquila-Natale, E. and Lamberti, L., 2019. What makes fashion consumers "click"? Generation of eWoM engagement in social media. *Asia Pacific Journal of Marketing and Logistics*, *31*(2), pp. 398–418.

Berger, A., Schlager, T., Sprott, D.E. and Hermann, A., 2018. Gamified interactions: Whether, when, and how games facilitate self-brand connections. *Journal of the Academy of Marketing Science*, *46*, pp. 652–673. https://doi.org/10.1007/s11747-017-0530-0.

Bhalla, R., 2014. The omni-channel customer experience: Driving engagement through digitisation. *Journal of Digital & Social Media Marketing*, *1*(4), pp. 365–372.

Castillo-Abdul, B., Pérez-Escoda, A. and Núñez-Barriopedro, E., 2022. Promoting social media engagement via branded content communication: A fashion brands study on Instagram. *Media and Communication*, *10*(1), pp. 185–197.

Deloitte, 2022. *The metaverse explained*. Deloitte. Available at: https://www2.deloitte.com/content/dam/Deloitte/us/Documents/mergers-acqisitions/user-friendly-the-metaverse-explained.pdf (Accessed: 20 March 2022).

De Valck, K., Van Bruggen, G.H. and Wierenga, B., 2009. Virtual communities: A marketing perspective. *Decision Support Systems*, *47*(3), pp. 185–203.

Ferrándiz, L., Fernández-Velilla, R. and Villanueva, J., 2016. *Social media marketing (SMM)*. MN-381-E, IESE Business School. Available at: https://www.iesepublishing.com/social-media-marketing-smm-english.html (Accessed: 23 March 2022).

García-San Miguel, J., 2017. *Hoja de Ruta: Transformación digital en el sector del retail textil*. IE Business school. Available at: https://landings.ie.edu/xlland-execed-es-hoja-ruta-transformacion-digital-textil (Accessed: 12 October 2022).

Hootsuite, 2022. *Social media trends 2022*. Hootsuite, 10 January. Available at: https://www.hootsuite.com/resources/blog/social-media-trends-2022 (Accessed: 23 February 2023).

Hootsuite and We Are Social Digital, 2022. *Digital 2022: Global overview report*. Hootsuite. Available at: https://wearesocial.com/cn/wp-content/uploads/sites/8/2022/01/DataReportal-GDR002-20220126-Digital-2022-Global-Overview-Report-Essentials-v02.pdf (Accessed: 23 March 2022).

Hubspot, 2022. *Social media trends*. Available at: https://www.hubspot.com/hubfs/EN%20Final%20SMT%20Report.pdf.

Kalbaska, N., Sádaba, T. and Cantoni, L., 2018. Fashion communication: Between tradition and digital transformation. *Studies in Communication Sciences*, *18*(2), pp. 269–285.

Kaplan, A.M. and Haenlein, M., 2010. Users of the world, unite! The challenges and opportunities of social media. *Business Horizons*, *53*(1), pp. 59–68.

Kontu, H. and Vecchi, A., 2014. Why all that noise-assessing the strategic value of social media for fashion brands. *Journal of Global Fashion Marketing*, *5*(3), pp. 235–250.

Liu, J. and Cantoni, L., 2023. European fashion companies and Chinese social media influencers: A "Liaison Dangereuse"? In *International conference on fashion communication: Between tradition and future digital developments* (pp. 124–135). Springer Nature.

Lu, B. and Chen, Z., 2021. Live streaming commerce and consumers' purchase intention: An uncertainty reduction perspective. *Information & Management*, *58*(7), p. 103509.

Lynch, S. and Barnes, L., 2020. Omnichannel fashion retailing: Examining the customer decision-making journey. *Journal of Fashion Marketing and Management: An International Journal*, *24*(3), pp. 471–493.

McKinsey, 2021. *Omnichannel: The path to value*. McKinsey. Available at: https://www.mckinsey.com/business-functions/marketing-and-sales/our-insights/the-survival-guide-to-omnichannel-and-the-path-to-value# (Accessed: 12 May 2022).

McKinsey and The Business of Fashion, 2022. *The state of fashion 2022*. McKinsey. Available at: https://www.mckinsey.com/~/media/mckinsey/industries/retail/our%20insights/state%20of%20fashion/2022/the-state-of-fashion-2022.pdf (Accessed: 12 March 2022).

Misopoulos, F., Mitic, M., Kapoulas, A. and Karapiperis, C., 2014. Uncovering customer service experiences with Twitter: The case of airline industry. *Management Decision*, *52*(4), pp. 705–723.

Nash, J., 2019. Exploring how social media platforms influence fashion consumer decisions in the UK retail sector. *Journal of Fashion Marketing and Management: An International Journal*, *23*(1), pp. 82–103.

Nobile, T.H. and Cantoni, L., 2022. Personalization and customization in fashion: Searching for a definition. *Journal of Fashion Marketing and Management: An International Journal*, *27*(4), pp. 665–682.

Nobile, T.H. and Cantoni, L., 2023. Personalisation (In)effectiveness in email marketing. *Digital Business*, *3*(2).

Noris, A., Sabatini, N. and Cantoni, L., 2023. Fashion games, fashion in games and gamification in fashion: A first map. In *International conference on human-computer interaction* (pp. 477–491). Springer Nature.

Portela, C., Kalbaska, N. and Cantoni, L., 2021. Omni-channel retailing in the fashion industry: Its definition and implementation. In *Fashion communication: Proceedings of the FACTUM 21 conference, Pamplona, Spain, 2021* (pp. 3–15). Springer International Publishing.

Roberts, J.A. and David, M.E., 2020. The social media party: Fear of missing out (FoMO), social media intensity, connection, and well-being. *International Journal of Human-Computer Interaction*, *36*(4), pp. 386–392.

Salaverría, R. and León, B., 2022. Misinformation beyond the media: "Fake news" in the big data ecosystem. In *Total journalism: Models, techniques and challenges* (pp. 109–121). Springer International Publishing.

SanMiguel, P., 2020. *Influencer marketing: Conecta tu marca con tu público*. Lid Editorial-Almuzara.

Scaraboto, D. and Fischer, E. 2013. Frustrated fatshionistas: An institutional theory perspective on consumer quests for greater choice in mainstream markets. *Journal of Consumer Research, 39*(6), pp. 1234–1257.

Thomas, L.J., Brooks, S. and McGouran, C., 2020. Antecedents of value co-creation activities for online fashion brands. *Journal of Strategic Marketing*, *28*(5), pp. 384–398.

TikTok, 2022. *Creator fund*. TikTok, 3 November. Available at: https://www.tiktok.com/creators/creator-portal/en-us/getting-paid-to-create/creator-fund/ (Accessed: 12 May 2022).

Tuten, T.L. and Solomon, M.R., 2018. *Social media marketing* (pp. 1–448). Sage Publications.

Vaughan, B. (2020). *Can niche communities replace social media?* WARC, 17 June. Available at: https://www.warc.com/newsandopinion/opinion/can-niche-communities-replace-social-media/en-gb/3674 (Accessed: 12 December 2023).

Voorveld, H.A., Van Noort, G., Muntinga, D.G. and Bronner, F., 2018. Engagement with social media and social media advertising: The differentiating role of platform type. *Journal of Advertising*, *47*(1), pp. 38–54.

WARC, 2021. *The WARC guide to brands and the creator economy*. WARC, 19 October. Available at: https://www.warc.com/content/paywall/article/bestprac/the-warc-guide-to-brands-and-the-creator-economy/en-gb/139253? (Accessed: 12 December 2023).

WARC, 2022. *The marketer's toolkit 2022*. WARC, 5 January. Available at: https://www.warc.com/content/paywall/article/warc-exclusive/the-marketers-toolkit-2022-global-trends-report/en-GB/140330 (Accessed: 3 February 2022).

Wongkitrungrueng, A., Dehouche, N. and Assarut, N., 2020. Live streaming commerce from the sellers' perspective: Implications for online relationship marketing. *Journal of Marketing Management*, *36*(5–6), pp. 488–518.

2

FASHION CONSUMER AND SOCIAL MEDIA

Introduction

The first objective of this chapter is to understand how social networks impact people's identity and behaviour. Moreover, it looks into how marketers can adopt such knowledge regarding digital identity to develop successful campaigns on social networks.

Second, this chapter introduces and explains the concept of segmentation. Segmentation is one of the essential parts of all marketing and communication plans. It involves the managers deciding whom to reach with the campaign messages. The decision taken at this stage affects the development of the entire campaign, including the design of the campaign, the tone of voice and the channels through which the campaign will be delivered.

Thanks to the developments of Information and Communication Technologies, segmentation processes have evolved a lot. Social networks allow companies to contact their consumers directly and reach specific users through tailored content. Therefore, micro-segmentation strategies can be developed through social networks.

As we will learn throughout this chapter, to carry out a correct segmentation, it is essential to have a deep and detailed knowledge of fashion social network users.

Digital Social Identity

We live in a hybrid world where online and offline realities are intertwined. Technology is transforming all social spheres: How we work, our relationships with others, how we make decisions, our shopping patterns and how we entertain ourselves. Mobile phones and smartphones have changed our lives by allowing virtual reality

DOI: 10.4324/9781003505495-4

to become part of our daily lives, making it easier to maintain our social relationships and overcome physical barriers (Chaffé and Smith, 2017; SanMiguel, 2020). By using mobile phones, social media users share an unprecedented volume of personal information, forming their digital social identity.

In order to understand digital social identity and its importance for fashion marketing and communication professionals, we must introduce three concepts: identity, self-identity and social identity.

According to the Oxford English Dictionary, *identity* is 'who or what somebody is,' *self-identity* is 'the way somebody considers their characteristics as a particular individual, especially in relation to the social environment they live or work in' and *social identity* is 'the part of the self-concept that derives from group membership". In other words, social identity can be defined as the self-concept that each individual makes of his/her 'self' in terms of the social groups to which the individual belongs, what he/she identifies with and how their self-esteem is created (Riva et al., 2016; Tuten and Solomon, 2018).

Through social networks, we share thoughts, opinions, activities, photos, videos, etc., and the platforms become part of our digital and real lives. As we have pointed out, social identity is the part of our self-concept that results from our perception of belonging to a group (Khajehelan, 2016; Pan et al., 2017). The identity-seeking behaviour of customers is one of the primary motivations for demonstrating online engagement behaviour through social media interaction (Farhat et al., 2021).

In social media networks, people belong to different social groups. The groups are formed by a set of users in a social network with common interests, for example, a group interested in fashion and lifestyles, brand fans or groups of followers, also called group membership, or a set of digital influencers. The interactions in these communities influence the way of being and behaving, ultimately building an individual's digital identity (Belentschikow et al., 2022; Shareef et al., 2020). 'Our online activities and the information we post document and express our social identity—the way we represent ourselves via our social connections, community membership, participation, and shared text, images, sounds, and video—to others who access the Web' (Tuten and Solomon, 2018, p. 45).

Users of social networks see their personal image being reflected in the brand's image (Farhat et al., 2021). Customers foster their social identity by associating with brands in this social relationship. Consumers form a brand perception based on the functional and symbolic benefits that are derived from the consumption of that brand. Therefore, social media is not only the place where brands can learn about consumers' social identity but also the place where they can shape it (Helal and Ozuem, 2018).

It is also interesting to note that in the same way that individuals shape their identity through social networks, they can also alter their own social identities through curated social media profiles to change how others perceive them (Riva et al., 2016).

Marketing professionals must be able to interpret consumers' digital identity and how social networks shape it. Indeed, an in-depth knowledge of the audience and consumers is essential to personalise the communication (Nobile and Cantoni, 2022, 2023; Nobile and Kalbaska, 2020).

Fashion eWOM and Conversations

Fashion functions as a language through which individuals express themselves and interact (Nobile et al., 2021), and the role of social media is crucial in this interaction. The presence of fashion brands on social networks is a key channel for the customer–brand connection (Noris et al., 2021).

As previously pointed out, our identity is shaped through conversations. These conversations powered by peer opinions and experiences generate e-Word of Mouth (eWOM), a beneficial source of information for understanding our consumers. This type of content can influence consumers' purchase intentions when the information obtained is of good quality, useful and credible (Leong et al., 2021). With the development and increased use of social networks, eWOM is also understood as non-textual communications such as 'liking' on Facebook, 'retweeting' on X (formerly known as Twitter) or a star rating on a review site. Due to the characteristics of the Internet, eWOM is becoming increasingly relevant since, in addition to the authority and trust granted by consumers, it is disseminated quickly, simply and unadorned (Ismagilova et al., 2021).

In fashion, Internet users share a great deal of advice on styling and buying clothes on social networks. People share their experiences on social networks due to the concern and desire to help others—especially friends and family—in their purchasing decisions (Hennig-Thurau, 2004).

In fashion, eWOM is a key recognition by consumers, which affects the buying process. eWOM is increasingly being seen by companies as a profitable and useful marketing tactic. Fashion consumers appreciate the social benefits of writing comments or sharing a post about a brand with a friend. Users rely on other consumers' opinions on social networks to evaluate purchase alternatives. They trust the opinions of their peers more than the information provided by the brand (SanMiguel and Sádaba, 2018).

Through social network conversations, fashion consumers can discover new trends, what their social group is wearing and accepting and where they can buy different garments and get the best deals. According to Parker and Kuo (2022), the motivations for sharing and consuming fashion-related content on social networks are:

- Associating with new fashion trends about new products and brands
- Participating in the fashion conversation,
- Seeking and giving fashion advice
- Having a close relationship with fashion brands

Fashion companies use social networks to foster direct and close customer conversations. The fashion company and the consumer can engage in conversations on a social platform with the same rules and tone. The consumer can ask the brands their questions, and the brands answer personally to their customers without the need for intermediaries (Wolny and Mueller, 2013).

Social networks have changed fashion companies' communication and marketing strategies, becoming one of the main tools for brand-building and advertising campaigns. Social networks also function as visual platforms where brands can convey their desired image, interact with opinion leaders and establish viral marketing strategies (Mohr, 2013).

Fashion Consumer: Analysis and Segmentation

For any fashion company, consumer knowledge is an essential part of its communication and marketing strategy success. Companies can perform segmentation through consumer analysis.

Segmentation divides customers into homogeneous groups with similar characteristics, preferences and needs (Melancon and Dalakas, 2018). Segmentation is the starting point of every marketing campaign and has been a central marketing concept for several decades (Pesonen, 2012). Groups or segments are defined on the basis of demographic details, behavioural habits, geographic location, interests and preferences (Dodson, 2016). In this book focused on social media management in fashion, we approach the analysis and segmentation of the consumer by considering:

1. Consumer characteristics
2. Behaviour on social networks
3. Behaviour as a fashion consumer

Consumer Characteristics

General segmentation, performed for all types of communication and marketing campaigns, is based on demographic, behavioural, psychographic, geographic and media habits characteristics (Narwal, 2019). Social networks offer multiple user data related to these characteristics. For example, the attributes that users provide about themselves on Facebook are used to obtain information and classify them according to the above categories: gender, relationship status, education status, age, location, language, interest and lifestyle. These characteristics allow brands to select and design the targeted campaigns.

Table 2.1 summarises consumer characteristics needed for further analysis and segmentation. The right column suggests possible sources, apart from the analytical tools of the social media platforms, from which consumer information can be extracted. It features various industry reports and statistical data sources.

TABLE 2.1 Consumer characteristics

Consumer	*Possible sources*
Demographic: Age Cultural background Educational level Ethnicity Gender Income Nationality Occupation Political affiliation Religion Social status	Consumer Barometer Demographics Pro Global Web Index National or Regional Statistical Offices Statista
Media habits (in general and specifically on social media): Time of the day that the consumer uses social media Platforms most commonly used Devices used to access social media	Bridge Ratings Media Research IAB Pew Research Similar Web SocialBakers Statista Think with Google WARC We are Social
Behavioural (Buying behaviour and decision-making): Brand interactions Customer loyalty Purchasing habits Spending habits	Online customer journey Statista WARC
Psychographic: Attitudes Interests and hobbies Lifestyle Motivations Personality Personal values Preferences and dislikes Psychological influences Subconscious and conscious beliefs	Global surveys of consumer sentiment (McKinsey, among others) WARC WGSN
Geographic: Location ZIP code City Country Radius around a specific location Climate Urban or rural	Company CRM Google Analytics Similar Web

Source: Own elaboration

Another way to segment social media uses is to consider the generation they belong to as this implies some of their characteristics and behaviours—for example whether they are millennials, Generation Z or Alpha. For example, let's suppose a user belongs to the millennials. In that case, their favourite networks are often Instagram or YouTube. If they are Alpha, they tend to prefer networks such as TikTok or Snapchat. Regarding the generations, it is preferable not to make strict generalisations about social media behaviour as this depends on various factors such as their country, lifestyle and individual preferences.

Behaviour on Social Networks

As we have seen in the first phase, one of the characteristics studied for communication and marketing plans is media habits. As this book focuses on social networks, we will investigate users' social network behaviour.

The data collected on social media allows us to get countless characteristics and behavioural aspects of users and consumers. By user social media behaviour, we understand users' behaviour in social networks, that is how they interact and why they interact based on their needs, interests and motivations.

The reasons why people use social networks are usually the following:

- To meet people or keep in touch
- To interact with the media, institutions and brands
- To share with people a look into their life
- To be informed on interesting information and content
- To be entertained, play games, engage in activities and stream music
- To follow trends and learn about new products and services

The behaviour of users on social networks can be analysed through their interaction with other users, brands and content. For example, how many followers they have, if they are active in publishing or consuming content, what type of content they like and share, etc. (Melancon and Dalakas, 2018; Tuten and Solomon, 2018).

In addition, the motivations that drive users to interact and participate constantly on social networks can help brands understand their social identity. Among the motivations (Tuten and Solomon, 2018, pp. 52–53), the following can be mentioned:

- Affinity impulse. Social networks enable participants to express an affinity, to acknowledge a liking and/or relationship with individuals and reference groups
- Personal utility impulse. The impulse that leads individuals to seek personal benefits
- Contact comfort and immediate impulse. People have a natural drive to feel a sense of psychological closeness to others. Contact comfort is the relief we feel from knowing that others in our network are accessible
- Altruistic impulse. Some participate in social media as a way to do something good. They use social media to 'make the world a better place'

- Curiosity impulse. The impulse to gain new knowledge and stimulate intellectual interests, epistemic curiosity is the driver
- Validation impulse. Social media focuses intently on the individual. You can share your opinions and activities as much as or as little as you like

Table 2.2 presents a classification of social network users based on their use and behaviour on social media.

Once marketers understand the types of motivations and how users express them, they can detect the specific motivations of their social media followers to

TABLE 2.2 Social media users' profile segmentation based on their behaviour

User profile	*Definition*
Information seeker	They seek information on diverse topics, especially in their areas of interest (e.g. fashion and beauty).
Help seeker	Users who seek advice on the Internet related to the products they want to buy, their hobbies, new fashion trends or how to use a face cream. They tend to follow many accounts due to their need to seek advice.
Advisor	People who advise on their profiles; although there are more and more users who give advice on all kinds of things related to their lives, on many occasions, the accounts with the most followers are those that consult on a certain topic, specialising in their knowledge and recommendations.
Social activist	Users who participate in conversations about topics of social interest and who frequently support social causes on social networks.
Entertainment seeker	They go to social networks mainly to entertain themselves; they like to watch videos and follow accounts that provide fun, entertaining content related to their hobbies.
Complainer	Those who use social networks as a channel to communicate their complaints or criticism of social issues, institutions and brands.
Active/Passive	People who actively participate in conversations, share content and interact with other accounts; or, on the contrary, users who consume content but do not interact or share.
Kind/Aggressive	Users who respect other accounts and content or who instead tend to communicate aggressively and disrespectfully.
Introverted/ Extroverted	Those people who share content related to their personal life and like to meet people through social networks or those more timid users who prefer not to share personal content and give more importance to their privacy.
Rational/ Emotional	Users who interact and share content rationally, thinking about each action they perform on social networks, or users who get carried away more by their emotions and impulses and interact more quickly and automatically.

Source: Profiles are based on Melancon and Dalakas (2018) and Tuten and Solomon (2018). The authors elaborated on the definitions of the profiles.

offer them a better experience, help them meet their needs and offer them relevant content. For example, if in the community of a fashion brand, the social media manager detects that a set of users have intrinsic motivations such as 'Contact comfort and immediacy impulse,' it will be convenient for the brand to respond to the comments that these users make on the content shared by the brand or at least 'like' the user's comment. Another example could be if the followers of a fashion brand belong to the behavioural group 'Entertainment seeker,' the brand's content creation team will have to address them by making the brand experience participatory or providing gaming content.

Behaviour as a Fashion Consumer

For this book, focused on the fashion industry, learning about fashion-related behaviour is essential. To understand the consumer behaviour in fashion, brands can ask themselves:

- Why do people want my product and brand?
- How does it make them feel?
- What does it do for them?
- What motivates them to choose my brand over another one?

It is also worth considering whether the brand is focused on a fashion consumer with a high fashion involvement and interest in fashion trends or sells products for consumers who are less interested in fashion trends and more interested in functionality.

Fashion involvement is a key motivation as many fashion consumers use social media to share their looks or content from events they participate in, that is they share their lifestyle (Solomon and Mrad, 2022). When consumers share their lives through an image, their clothes and style are the strongest communication language. In other words, even if users share content that is not about fashion, fashion is present, communicating tangible and intangible aspects of that person (Sabatini and Cantoni, 2023). Also, discovery is an essential motivation for fashion lovers; through social networks, consumers can learn about new brands and fashion trends, keep abreast of new collections, interact with brands worldwide and be part of their communities. Related to discovery is inspiration social networks, especially Instagram and Pinterest, which group an infinite amount of content that inspires the style of millions of people, content created by brands, by users and by content creators or influencers specialised in fashion (Gretzel, 2023).

In Table 2.3, we will look at six fashion consumer profiles while considering their motivations and behaviour.

With all the information analysed and taking into account the possible segmentations in the three perspectives explained (consumer characteristics, behaviour on social networks and behaviour as a fashion consumer), brands can create

TABLE 2.3 Profile of fashion consumers based on motivations and behaviour

Fashion consumers and lifestyle groups	*Motivation and behaviour*
Grab a Bargain	• Consumers buy in sales • Attracted by promotional offers • Buy vintage or second-hand • Go to designer outlets or clearance sales • Collect discount vouchers or coupons
Stand Out from the Crowd	• Consumers shop in independent shops • Strive to seek out new trends and ideas • Make their clothes or personalise them • Shop at street markets
Social Fitting In and Belonging	• Buy styles similar to those of their friends • Ask like-minded people where they usually shop for fashion
Avoiding Shopping	• Consumers do not buy clothes frequently • Purchase mainly replacement items • Do not browse around the shop but go directly to the item in question • Leave the shop if the queue to pay is too long
Looking Like Celebrities	• Consumers follow celebrities in the media • They are attracted to shop what celebrities shop • Would queue up to buy fashion collections from certain celebrities or designers
Lifestyle	• Fashionistas: Consumers looking for the latest fashion trends • Forever young: Consumers looking for youth fashion brands and youthful looks • Wellness lover: Consumers looking for comfortable looks and sportswear fabrics • Classic: Consumer looking for classic brands, looks and styles and basic products and colours

Source: Based on Harriet Posner (2015, p. 117) and Everis (2018)

profiles that describe their customers, the so-called Buyer Personas. The concept of the buyer persona and how it can be analysed and created will be explained in Chapter 3, *Social Media Strategy*.

Bibliography

Belentschikow, V., Pfeffel, K. and Müller, N.H., 2022. Making friends on Facebook: Common group membership as a central decision rule. *Computers in Human Behavior*, *126*, p. 107040.

Chaffé, D. and Smith, P.R., 2017. *Digital marketing excellence: Planning, optimization and integrating online marketing*. Routledge.

Dodson, I., 2016. *The art of digital marketing: The definitive guide to creating strategic, targeted, and measurable online campaigns*. John Wiley & Sons.

Everis Report, 2018. *Tendencias de consumo en fashion retail*. ISEM Fashion School.

Farhat, K., Aslam, W. and Mokhtar, S.S.M., 2021. Beyond social media engagement: Holistic digital engagement and a social identity perspective. *Journal of Internet Commerce*, *20*(3), pp. 319–354.
Gretzel, U., 2023. Tourism and fashion influencers: Comparison of visual practices. In *Fashion and tourism: Parallel stories* (Vol. 26, pp. 47–58). Emerald Publishing Limited.
Helal, G. and Ozuem, W., 2018. Social identity matters: Social media and brand perceptions in the fashion apparel and accessories industries. In *Digital marketing strategies for fashion and luxury brands* (pp. 326–361). IGI Global.
Hennig-Thurau, T., 2004. Customer orientation of service employees: Its impact on customer satisfaction, commitment, and retention. *International Journal of Service Industry Management*, *15*(5), pp. 460–478.
Ismagilova, E., Rana, N.P., Slade, E.L. and Dwivedi, Y.K., 2021. A meta-analysis of the factors affecting eWOM providing behaviour. *European Journal of Marketing*, *55*(4), pp. 1067–1102.
Khajeheian, D., 2016. Intercultural peers' effect on social identity of social media users: A critical study of consumer socialization theory. *Journal of Business and Economics*, *7*(3), pp. 467–473.
Leong, C.M., Loi, A.M.W. and Woon, S., 2021. The influence of social media eWOM information on purchase intention. *Journal of Marketing Analytics*, pp. 1–13.
Narwal, N., 2019. Customer segmentation using social media data. *International Journal of Management, IT and Engineering*, *7*(10), 117–125.
Nobile, T.H. and Cantoni, L., 2022. Personalization and customization in fashion: Searching for a definition. *Journal of Fashion Marketing and Management: An International Journal*, *27*(4), pp. 665–682.
Nobile, T.H. and Cantoni, L., 2023. Personalisation (in)effectiveness in email marketing. *Digital Business*, *3*(2).
Nobile, T.H. and Kalbaska, N., 2020. An exploration of personalization in digital communication. insights in fashion. In *HCI in business, government and organizations: 7th international conference, HCIBGO 2020, held as Part of the 22nd HCI international conference, HCII 2020, Copenhagen, Denmark, July 19–24, 2020, Proceedings 22* (pp. 456–473). Springer International Publishing.
Nobile, T.H., Noris, A., Kalbaska, N. and Cantoni, L., 2021. A review of digital fashion research: Before and beyond communication and marketing. *International Journal of Fashion Design, Technology and Education*, *14*(3), pp. 293–301.
Noris, A., Nobile, T.H., Kalbaska, N. and Cantoni, L., 2021. Digital fashion: A systematic literature review. A perspective on marketing and communication. *Journal of Global Fashion Marketing*, *12*(1), pp. 32–46.
Melancon, J.P. and Dalakas, V., 2018. Consumer social voice in the age of social media: Segmentation profiles and relationship marketing strategies. *Business Horizons*, *61*(1), pp. 157–167.
Mohr, I., 2013. The impact of social media on the fashion industry. *Journal of Applied Business and Economics*, *15*(2), pp. 17–22.
Pan, Z., Lu, Y., Wang, B. and Chau, P.Y., 2017. Who do you think you are? Common and differential effects of social self-identity on social media usage. *Journal of Management Information Systems*, *34*(1), pp. 71–101.
Parker, C.J. and Kuo, H.Y., 2022. What drives generation-y women to buy fashion items online? *Journal of Marketing Theory and Practice*, *30*(3), pp. 279–294.
Pesonen, J., 2012. Social media channel segmentation of tourists. *e-Review of Tourism Research (eRTR)*, *10*(2), pp. 67–71.
Posner, H., 2015. *Marketing fashion second edition: Strategy, branding and promotion*. Laurence King Publishing.
Riva, G., Wiederhold, B.K. and Cipresso, P., 2016. Psychology of social media: From technology to identity. In *The psychology of social networking* (Vol. 1, pp. 4–14). De Gruyter Open Poland.

Sabatini, N. and Cantoni, L., 2023. Linking fashion and tourism: From body to clothing and lifestyle. In *Fashion and tourism: Parallel stories* (pp. 33–46). Emerald Publishing Limited.

SanMiguel, P., 2020. *Influencer marketing: Conecta tu marca con tu público*. Editorial Almuzara.

SanMiguel, P. and Sádaba, T., 2018. Nice to be a fashion blogger, hard to be influential: An analysis based on personal characteristics, knowledge criteria, and social factors. *Journal of Global Fashion Marketing*, *9*(1), pp. 40–58.

Shareef, M.A., Kapoor, K.K., Mukerji, B., Dwivedi, R. and Dwivedi, Y.K., 2020. Group behavior in social media: Antecedents of initial trust formation. *Computers in Human Behavior*, *105*, p. 106225.

Solomon, M.R. and Mrad, M., 2022. *Fashion & luxury marketing*. Sage Publications.

Tuten, T.L. and Solomon, M.R., 2018. *Social media marketing* (pp. 1–448). Sage Publications.

Wolny, J. and Mueller, C., 2013. Analysis of fashion consumers' motives to engage in electronic word-of-mouth communication through social media platforms. *Journal of Marketing Management*, *29*(5–6), pp. 562–583.

SECTION 2

Social Media Strategy and Plan

In this section, we will present the steps for developing a social media strategy. We will discuss the relevance of conducting an internal and external diagnosis to make strategic decisions that will make your social media mix planning coherent and effective.

This section consists of two chapters.

- Chapter 3, ***Social Media Strategy***, addresses the main ideas for carrying out a situation analysis from both the internal point of view, where a social media audit is highly relevant, and from an external point of view, where it is necessary to take into account the behaviour of the competition, the market trends and the needs and motivations of the target audience. The chapter discusses how to understand objectives, define the social media persona and decide the strategic message and tone of voice. These steps are essential to develop a coherent social media strategy.
- Chapter 4, ***Social Media Mix Planning,*** highlights the importance of selecting social media channels strategically. It analyses the peculiarities of the social media marketing mix.

After reading this section, you will:

- Understand the relevance of developing a situation analysis considering the internal situation and the external environment (competitors, market trends and target audience)
- Learn how to conduct a social media audit for internal analysis and to compare your performance to that of one of your competitors

DOI: 10.4324/9781003505495-5

- Be able to explain the essential elements on which the social media plan should be based, such as objectives, social media persona, strategic message and tone of voice
- Learn how to make strategic decisions for designing the social media marketing mix

3

SOCIAL MEDIA STRATEGY

Introduction

In order to start developing a social media strategy, it is necessary to conduct a *situation analysis*. Professionals from Smart Insights, Chaffey and Smith (2012) created the *SOSTAC planning framework* applied to digital marketing strategy development, which covers situation analysis, objectives, strategy, tactics, actions and control by comprehensively answering these questions:

- Where are we now?
- Where do we want to be?
- How do we get there?
- How exactly do we get there?
- Who does what and when?
- How do we monitor performance?

In this chapter, we will focus on the company's internal aspects regarding its marketing strategy and previous social media activity (such as social media audit). Then, we will incorporate essential information required in an external environment analysis regarding the competitors and trends and the consumers. In Chapter 2, a rigorous explanation of the main aspects you have to consider to understand fashion consumers in social media can be found. Thus, in this chapter, this content will not be repeated, although the research about consumers, both qualitative and quantitative, is essential in preparing a social media plan.

DOI: 10.4324/9781003505495-6

Social Media Audit

We will start from the internal point of view. In this part, it is essential to analyse and consider answering the following questions:

- What is the connection between your company's social media actions and marketing objectives?
- How prepared is the company to develop its social media strategy? What is its knowledge and understanding of social media? What resources does the company have to develop a social media strategy?
- How is it positioned in the market? Which brand values are present in the different communication channels? Which consumers it wants to reach, and through which social networks?

Sutherland (2021, p. 19) suggests valuable questions for social media consultants to ask their clients to understand their attitude towards consumers, competitors and previous social media activities:

1. When and why did you start your business?
2. What are your products and services?
3. What are your business goals?
4. What is your greatest challenge in achieving those goals?
5. What are the best and most challenging things about your industry?
6. Who are your customers? Who would you like them to be?
7. How would you rate your current customer experience and service?
8. How would (and have) your customers rated their experience with your business?
9. What are some of your common customer complaints?
10. What are some of your customer's common questions?
11. Who are your direct competitors?
12. Do you have branding guidelines?
13. What are your current social media activities?
14. What has been successful and unsuccessful for you on social media?
15. What do you want social media to do for your business?

After answering these questions, we should prepare *a social media audit,* which involves a complete analysis of a client's social media activities and performance (Quesenberry, 2016; Sutherland, 2021; Tuten and Solomon, 2017). In Table 3.1, we will introduce some of the main questions that should be answered while preparing a social media audit.

Competitor and Social Media Trends Analysis

Several aspects of the competition must be studied, including an understanding of global marketing and communication strategy and an overview of their social media activities.

TABLE 3.1 Social media audit for internal analysis

Social media audit	*Suggested points to evaluate and questions to answer*
Geography and localisation	In which language the communication is done? The start/end date of the profile/campaign Use of geoinformation: Identify if the company uses geolocations or if the updates are posted in a specific country or city
Visual representation of the brand on each social media profile	How is the client visually representing their brand on each of their social media profiles? If they are using or not: The correct logo, the correct brand colours, images that adhere to the size specifications of the specific social media platforms, images that are of high enough resolutions, using copyright-free and royalty-free images, visual imagery that looks professional and is identifiable as their brand.
Textual representation of the brand on each social media profile	Are bio sections on each profile populated? Is the company information up to date? Does the company info leverage the features of the platform? Is the current text free from errors of spelling, grammar and punctuation? Does the text truly capture the organisation's brand voice? Has the bio been written with the target audience in mind? What text is missing from social media profiles that could help the target audience learn more about a client's business?
Previous social media activity	Frequency of posts Days and times the content is being posted Types of content posted What type of creative content works best; For example video, photo, carousel? Quality of content posted Relevance of the platform Originality of content Alignment to brand and brand voice Relevance to the audience Demographics and gender targeting Placement and device performing of ads Campaign performance and organic performance Location targeting Use of hashtags
Social media performance Indicators of content interaction	Data from each platform's analytics Month-over-month and year-over-year performance Number of followers and page likes Reach Engagement Content generating the most significant audience response
Conversion metrics	Google analytics data Social media promotions converting to in-store sales Event attendance as a result of social media promotion Social media driving online registration Social media attracting donations and volunteers

Source: Own elaboration based on Sutherland (2021), pp. 19–23; Hubspot (2022)

Useful components to guide a competitor analysis are:

- Social media platforms used by each competitor
- Number of social media profiles
- Page likes and follower numbers across platforms
- Visual and textual representation of the brand on social media profiles
- Social media activity
- Types of content
- Audience engagement
- Share of voice analysis

In a simpler way, Quesenberry (2016, p. 65) proposes the following template (Table 3.2), taking into account the 5w's from journalists:

This type of competitor analysis is called the social media benchmark analysis, which is a systematic and objective way to evaluate and compare a brand's performance on social media with other similar players. The social media benchmark can be done by comparing different brands and evaluating the performance of specific campaigns. In this way, best and worst industry practices can be identified. Finally, after finding the gaps in a company's social media marketing strategy, the companies gain ideas for ways to differentiate/improve their communication strategy.

Subsequently, we must identify the main social, cultural, legal, political, economic and technological trends that could affect the decisions to be taken in social media strategy.

It is also relevant to analyse the trends of social networks themselves: How they are evolving, how the algorithm is updated in each of them, what advances they are allowing and how they can be used for marketing objectives, etc. It is essential to be constantly updated on these issues. In Table 3.3, there is an example of some important sources of information.

After having collected all the relevant information, it is essential to apply diagnosis tools to reach insights and make strategic decisions. A possible tool is the *SWOT analysis*, which helps us identify, from an internal and external point of view, the strengths, weaknesses, threats and opportunities that the brand has at a given time in designing a social media strategy.

TABLE 3.2 Competitors' social media audit (or benchmark analysis)

Who	*Where (channel/ environment)*	*What (content/ sentiment)*	*When (data/frequency)*	*Why (purpose/ performance)*
Your company				
Competitors				

Source: Own elaboration based on Quesenberry (2016)

TABLE 3.3 Suggestions of topics and sources related to social media trends

Cultural trends	*Social media trends*	*Content trends*	*Fashion trends*
Cassandra Daily	Hootsuite	Content Marketing Institute	Fashion United
Google Trends	Hubspot		The Business of Fashion
Hofstede Insights	IAB		Trend Hunter
Intelligence	SemRush		Vogue Business
Our World in Data			WGSN
PSFK			
Report Linker			
TED Talks			
Trend Hunter			
Trend Watching			
Think with Google			
Wunderman Thompson			
YouTube Culture & Trends			
YPulse			

Source: Own elaboration

Social Media Marketing Strategy

After having analysed the internal and external information, brands can develop a social media strategy as a formalised orientation framework that sets goals and describes how the company and its customers will collaborate to achieve goals, as well as how each social media network should be used and integrated to support the main objective of the company (Marchand et al., 2021, p. 552).

It is not enough just to be present on social networks; it is essential to adopt a strategic, comprehensive and coherent approach so that social networks are integrated into a company's marketing plan.

Felix et al. (2017, p. 120) propose a holistic framework to understand social media strategically. They explain it as follows:

- First, the scope of social media marketing addresses the question of how companies use social media marketing. Defenders use social media marketing primarily as a one-way communication tool to entertain consumers or to inform stakeholders. In contrast, explorers are interested in an authentic social media marketing collaboration based on reciprocal interactions with many stakeholders such as clients, employees, suppliers and government agents.
- Second, social media marketing culture distinguishes between conservatism, represented by an encapsulated, traditional and mass advertising approach, and modernism, characterised by a more permeable, open and flexible social media marketing culture.
- Third, the social media marketing structure addresses the organisation and departmentalisation of the firm's social media marketing assignment. Hierarchies

stand for a centralised approach with a clearly defined social media marketing assignee. Networks represent an organisational structure in which all employees are responsible for social media marketing; thus, a dedicated social media marketing director is no longer necessary.

- Fourth, social media marketing governance refers to how the company establishes rules and guidelines and how social media marketing responsibilities are controlled. The extreme position of autocracy describes a situation with precise regulations on who in the company is allowed to interact on social media platforms. Conversely, anarchy represents a situation without any rules or guidelines.

The concept of strategic maturity in the use of social networks, as proposed by Tuten and Solomon (2018), illustrates how organisations evolve in their approach to social media marketing. This process unfolds through three distinct phases: trial, transition and strategic.

In the trial phase, companies begin experimenting with social media platforms. This stage is characterised as a period of initial exploration, where the emphasis is more on initial trials rather than on integrating social media into the company's overall marketing strategy. Subsequently, organisations progress to the transition phase. Here, they adopt a more systematic approach to social media marketing, though they have not yet achieved a fully strategic approach. Finally, in the strategic phase, social media is cohesively integrated into the organisation's overall marketing plan. In this advanced stage, companies implement a formal process for planning and executing social media marketing activities, establishing clear objectives and measurable metrics to assess performance.

This model is crucial for understanding how companies can more effectively utilise social media as they grow in their strategic maturity. It underscores the need for organisations to evolve from merely using social media as an engagement tool to integrating it as a key component in their overall marketing strategy.

Li et al. (2021, pp. 61–62) propose different levels of strategic maturity related to their engagement with social media. Although they do not follow a sequential pattern, their success will be determined by the firm's strategic objectives, resources and capabilities:

- Social commerce strategy (to promote and sell): Social media as a selling, promotion and advertising platform has a positive impact on customer purchase intentions and financial performance.
- Social content strategy (to connect and collaborate): Content popularity and vitality are influenced by social message strategy, seeding strategy and context, product characteristics, organisational processes and IT tools.
- Social monitoring strategy (to listen and learn): Emphasises the importance of social listening and responding to customer needs.

- Social CRM strategy (to empower and engage): Customer engagement and social CRM capabilities affect the core of social CRM strategy, which positively affects competitive advantage and performance.

In a social media marketing strategy, brands have to work on different areas: The main goals and objectives of the social media strategy, social media persona and the strategic message. All the elements will be presented in depth below.

Defining Goals and Objectives

We can differentiate short-term or long-term strategies related to social media management. Short-term strategies put the emphasis on supporting certain social media activities at a specific moment, for example, an event, fashion show, collection launch, etc. On the other hand, ongoing or long-term strategies seek the day-to-day continuity of social media activities that support the achievement of overall business goals. It is important that a brand knows how to manage both types of objectives, and all of them must have a clear strategic coherence even if the temporal effect is different. In fact, short-term strategies can be integrated into longer and day to day strategies.

With these ideas in mind, we can differentiate between goals and objectives. A goal is the most preferred outcome a client or an organisation intends to achieve.

While the goals have a general and broad view of what the brand expects from social media, the objectives add specific details to know how to achieve them. Following Tuten and Solomon (2018, p. 200), 'an objective is a specific statement about a planned social media activity in terms of what that activity intends to accomplish.' The objective will vary based on the situation, and the problem might be based on the general marketing objectives. Communication and marketing objectives by fashion companies must be perfectly related and coherent among all the brand's communication and sales channels so that customers and users perceive a coherent message.

In Table 3.4, we include the main five phases of the marketing funnel that include specific goals that are relevant to social media campaigns.

In order to clarify how the objectives are connected, Table 3.5 provides several concrete examples.

Besides, it should be remembered that objectives must be SMART (Chaffey and Ellis-Chadwick, 2019, p. 156):

- Specific: Is the objective sufficiently detailed to measure real-world problems and opportunities?
- Measurable: Can a quantitative and qualitative attribute be applied to create a metric?
- Actionable: Can the information be used to improve the performance?

TABLE 3.4 Main social media marketing goals

Objectives	*Definition*	*Main outputs*
Awareness	To make our clients aware of our brand or product	Ad recall Brand lift
Consideration	To give an opportunity to the clients to compare different options	Website visits Engagement
Conversion	To make clients purchase, start a trial or become a lead for our sales	Conversions Purchases Leads
Loyalty	To make sure that our customers are satisfied with the product and remain with the brand	Upselling Cross-selling
Advocacy	To make our clients the ambassadors for our brand through word-of-mouth	Social proof Credibility

Source: Own elaboration

TABLE 3.5 Objectives for social media campaigns of fashion brands

Business objectives	*Marketing objectives*	*Social media objectives*
Enter the North European market with the current product range. Increase market share.	Increase awareness in those countries. Target professional and young women.	Communicate all the news of the brand and its products on Instagram and Pinterest. Drive engagement through impactful content. Increase the number of followers and users who interact with the brand profile.

Source: Own elaboration

- Relevant: Can the information be applied to the specific problem faced by the manager?
- Time-related: Can the information be constrained through time?

An example of SMART objectives for the 'Increasing brand awareness' goal could be the following:

- Specific: State how much awareness among a target market is expected to increase—for example 10%.
- Measurable: Measure current awareness level and plan to collect awareness levels later.
- Achievable: Is a 10% increase feasible?
- Relevant: How is the increase relevant? Can we eventually cope with such an increase?
- Time-related: Set a due date—for example in 2 months.

During the realisation of digital marketing plans, professionals should always measure how the campaign is performing and the actions they are carrying out, before, during and after. For this reason, the objectives are usually presented together with their KPIs.

Table 3.6 presents an outline of the path that can be followed by social media marketing professionals when designing their actions. It proposes a series of examples from the moment a brand reflects on its general marketing objectives, such as brand awareness, consideration, conversion and loyalty, to the specific social media objectives, possible actions that could achieve each of the objectives and their corresponding KPIs. Therefore, the next steps should be followed:

1. Define marketing objectives
2. Set specific objectives
3. Select KPIs for monitoring the marketing objectives
4. Select the objectives in social networks
5. Set KPIs for monitoring the actions in social networks

Social Media Persona

Once we have defined the objectives of our social media campaign, we must define specifically what type of persona our social media strategy is going to approach. To do this, we can use the 'persona methodology.'

Personas are fictional characters created to represent the different types of users with various attitudes and behaviours of a hypothetical group of users. Personas are used to classify the behaviour patterns, goals, skills, abilities, attitudes, hopes, needs and environment of a potential user of the product or service. Personas are a tool for analysing qualitative user-research material. They function as an inspirational resource during the strategic process.

Even though the personas themselves may be fictional, the motivations and reactions they exhibit are real. Personas represent the feedback elicited during the social media audit and as such embody the real-world perceptions surrounding a company's service.

The personas can be created by reviewing secondary sources and through in-depth interviews with consumers. For in-depth interviews with consumers, the following steps can be followed as a guide:

- Interview and/or observation of an adequate number of people.
- Find patterns in the interviewees' responses and actions, and use those to group similar respondents together.
- Create archetypical models of those groups based on the patterns found.
- Use the information collected to create the personas.
- Share the personas with other team members and stakeholders.
- Design your social media strategy, having the personas at the centre.

Table 3.7 presents an example of how a Fashion Social Media Buyer Persona profile can look like.

TABLE 3.6 Specific social media objectives, social media actions, KPIs

	Brand awareness	*Consideration*	*Conversion*	*Loyalty and advocacy*
Specific Social Media Objective	Communicate all the news of the brand and its products. Share the history of the brand. Increase the number of followers and users who interact with the brand profile. Actively listen to the community. Know the desires and needs of users in social networks. Know the social sentiment in the brand community and influence it.	Generate website traffic through social media. Increase the number of active followers. Generate conversations. Increase interactions with content. Improve engagement rates on the social profile. Get users to share brand content.	Generate leads. Generate sales on the social network. Generate sales that finance on the web. Increase the community. Take care of customer service, before and during the purchase.	Encourage membership in the community of followers and the transformation of followers into prescribers. Encourage followers to share content and share their experiences. Take care of customer service. Encourage the generation of user content with our products.
Social Media Actions	Transmit the story and brand values through publications. Follow up and conversate with relevant hashtags for the brand and product. Use keywords in the texts published in social networks to improve brand positioning, especially in those social networks where Google tags their content. Social sentiment analysis about the brand and related topics.	Share the content of interest that arouses the desire to be read in its full version on the web. Share product photos. Share photos of events. Sharing videos of collections. Presentation of campaigns. Live videos showing the products and the brand's staff. Post conversation topics in the community of followers. Respond to user comments on social networks.	Share the promotions. Share the product pages for direct sales. Create a product showcase. Create contests on your social media profiles for your visitors and followers to participate in. Sell your products through your social profiles.	Take care of the community. Respond to their direct messages and comments. Interact with the content users share by mentioning the brand while being grateful. Reward users who share more content about the brand. Address possible conversations that provide a negative view of the brand or product. Measure brand sentiment. Make exclusive actions for key users of the brand.

(*Continued*)

TABLE 3.6 (Continued)

	Brand awareness	*Consideration*	*Conversion*	*Loyalty and advocacy*
	Share the content with trending hashtags to reach new audiences. Collaborate with influencers or opinion leaders in social networks to amplify brand content. Communicate in social media the participation of the brand in events related to the brand/product to raise brand awareness. Share links that redirect to the website.	Include links to your website and offers in the bio sections of your profiles. Create contests together with other brands to reach new audiences. Measure and participate in relevant hashtags for each campaign. Participate in social movements and dates. Involve users in the design or production process of the brand's products.	Carry out specific promotions, taking into account the brand's promotion calendar. Answer specific questions from followers about products. Share special or promotional products through influencers.	
Social Media KPIs	Like posts. Like the page. Comments. Shared content. Scope of our publications. Number of impressions. Views of profiles, photos and videos. Brand mentions.	The traffic to the web coming from social networks is analysed. How those visitors are like: Their page views, unique or recurring visits or the follow-up of those visits. Likes. Followers. Comments. Favourites. Saved. Retweets. Engagement rates. Shared. Web link clicks.	Number of followers and degree of community interaction. Downloads of social media content. Application of promotions or discount codes disseminated by the social media. Number of transactions carried out. Conversion of social media advertising. Average number of consumers coming from social media.	Active life of users and consumers. Responses to users' questions or doubts in social networks. Response on time. Degree of user satisfaction after the response.

Source: Own elaboration

TABLE 3.7 Fashion social media buyer persona example

Age	23
Gender	Female
Location	Boston, the United States
Living situation	Renting an apartment with a friend
Hobbies	Walking dog, hanging out with friends, eating at restaurants, following fashion
Job title	MIT student and retail assistant
Influencers they follow	@emmahill, @chiaraferragni, @blancamiro
Fashion brands they follow	@dior, @andotherstories, @zara, @prada
Hashtags they engage with	#style, #fashion, #OOTD
Personality	Outgoing, ambitious, fashionable
Active social media channels	Instagram, YouTube
Preferred content types	Instagram Reels, YouTube videos, Instagram Story polls
Social media user	Information seeker, entertainment seeker, active and extrovert user
Goals and motivations	Grow her own Instagram account, become a fashion influencer and eventually open her own fashion store in LA
Fears and pain points	She can't afford high-quality clothing because her job doesn't pay well, and she's paying rent in an expensive part of town
Buying triggers	Seeing friends or influencers with fashion items she doesn't have

Source: Own elaboration

Social Media Value Proposition

Once the brand has focused on the objectives it wants to achieve and it has well-defined the type of consumer it wants to reach, it is necessary to specify the strategic positioning it wants to adopt along all the social media campaigns. This should flow from the brand's positioning statement—

> [A] single written statement that encapsulates the position the brand wishes to hold in the minds of its target audience. Positioning statements succinctly capture the heart of what the brand is. Reviewing the position is necessary in preparing a social media marketing strategy because the social media activities the campaign plans and executes need to support the desired message consistently.
>
> *(Tuten and Solomon, p. 122)*

It is interesting to quote the *Golden Circle* in order to build on the purpose and essence of the brand. Sinek explains this model in his book *Start with Why* (2009). The 'Why' is the most important message that the company can communicate about itself, and it should inspire everything it does. Therefore, it is essential to work from:

- *Why*: The purpose, the motivation, what do you believe in as a company?

- *How*: The process, specific actions taken to realise the 'Why'
- *What*: The result of the 'Why'—proof

In communication, we talk about defining the value proposition, considering the brand's values and how they connect with the specific consumers you want to reach. In this sense, it is necessary to move from the Online Value Proposition (what differentiates your brand from other brands in the online environment) to the *Social Media Value Proposition*: Among all the fashion brands that consumers find on social networks, what makes your brand different?

This Social Media Value Proposition must be specified in some *key messages*, which are the most important points of information to communicate to the target audience, and they must be succinct, clear and uncomplicated. They must be created with social media personas in mind so that they are understandable and relevant to them. All subsequent content should be based on these strategically delineated key messages. Sutherland (2021) argues how a key message generally aims to fulfil one of the following functions in communicating with a target audience: To inform, educate, establish empathy, solve problems or inspire action. Sutherland suggests six strategic key questions (Table 3.8) to evaluate whether our key messages are strategically well-defined.

Taking into account this Social Media Value Proposition, we must also decide, from a strategic point of view, the tone of voice of the communication, the personality of the brand that should be portrayed and the style of publications in the different media used. The selection of the different channels is a strategic aspect which should be based on thorough consumer research. It will be discussed in detail in the next chapter of the book.

An issue that is also strategic and, therefore, has to be well defined in this part is the type of *experience* that the brand wants to develop with consumers: What do we want consumers to do from our actions in social media?

The strategy should be summarised in a document called *social media marketing briefing*. It should include the most relevant aspects that the employees who will implement it should know and remember while implementing the social media campaigns (Table 3.9).

TABLE 3.8 Key questions to develop strategic messages

1. What is the most important information that the audience needs to know to support the achievement of the strategic goals and SMART objectives?
2. What doesn't the audience need to know?
3. How will the target audience benefit from the knowledge in this key message?
4. What is the specific problem experienced by the target audience, and how can we provide a solution?
5. Clearly state the actions you want the target audience to undertake. What is the call to action?
6. What will the target audience gain from performing the call-to-action?

Source: Sutherland (2021, pp. 87–88)

TABLE 3.9 Guide for social media marketing briefing

What are the campaign goals and/or communication objectives?
What are the campaign's social media objectives?
How is the brand positioned? What is unique and special about its position in the marketplace?
What are the key messages?
Who is the target audience (social media personas), and what do you want the audience to do on your social media profiles?
Is there another group of people who can persuade the target audience to follow them? This group is your influencers—the people who will propagate your message. Why would these people want to share your message with others? What's in it for them?
How can we integrate with other branded media being used by the organisation, and how long do we have to execute?
What experiences are possible, given the target market needs and motivations and our available channels? How can we design these experiences to maximise device portability and access?
What content will be needed? What content will be relevant to the campaign, and what will be the source?
How will experience engagement be extended and shared throughout the social channels?

Source: Own elaboration based on Tuten and Solomon (2018)

Bibliography

Chaffey, D. and Ellis-Chadwick, F., 2019. *Digital marketing*. Pearson.

Chaffey, D. and Smith, P., 2012. *SOSTAC marketing planning model guide*. Smartinsights, 27 April. Available at: https://www.smartinsights.com/digital-marketing-strategy/sostac-model/ (Accessed: 13 May 2022).

Felix, R., Rauschnabel, P.A. and Hinsch, C., 2017. Elements of strategic social media marketing: A holistic framework. *Journal of Business Research*, *70*, pp. 118–126.

Hubspot, 2022. *How to conduct a social media audit*. Hubspot, 26 January. Available at: https://blog.hubspot.com/customers/check-pulse-digital-strategy-social-media-audit (Accessed: 28 October 2022).

Li, F., Larimo, J. and Leonidou, L.C., 2021. Social media marketing strategy: Definition, conceptualization, taxonomy, validation, and future agenda. *Journal of the Academy of Marketing Science*, *49*, pp. 51–70.

Marchand, A., Hennig-Thurau, T. and Flemming, J., 2021. Social media resources and capabilities as strategic determinants of social media performance. *International Journal of Research in Marketing*, *38*(3), pp. 549–571.

Quesenberry, K.A., 2016. *Social media strategy: Marketing, advertising, and public relations in the consumer revolution*. Rowman & Littlefield Publishers.

Sinek, S., 2009. *Start with why* (pp. 1–256). Penguin.

Sutherland, K.E., 2021. *Strategic social media management: Theory and practice*. Springer Nature.

Tuten, T.L. and Solomon, M.R., 2017. *Social media marketing* (pp. 1–448). Sage Publications.

4

SOCIAL MEDIA MIX PLANNING

Introduction

This chapter explains how to carry out a social media mix plan. Starting from the strategy, the plan describes how the objectives of the social media campaign will be achieved. First, the characteristics of social media platforms and how they can be utilised to reach the company's social media persona (or the so-called 'campaign's target group') are discussed. Subsequently, it explains how to combine the different channels and content, what we call the social media mix.

Each social media network is a channel to communicate and interact with consumers and sell products. There may be consumers who follow the same brand on different social platforms or consumers who may only follow the brand on a specific social network. Hence, consistency in the brand's messaging and communication is crucial. Moreover, each social network has its own characteristics and operations that must be taken into consideration. Social media professionals need to have a broad understanding of the different channels and their characteristics:

- How the algorithm works
- How the API[1] is functioning
- Type of content that can be offered in the profiles
- Predominant audience characteristics
- Hours of the highest concentration of interactions
- Specifications of the content that can be published
- Advertising formats
- Facilitating marketing tools such as the business pages of each social network
- KPIs and measurement metrics

DOI: 10.4324/9781003505495-7

Social Media Platform Characteristics

The objective of this chapter is to understand the main features of the different social networks and their implications on fashion marketing plans. Knowing them is critical to be able to strategically decide through which channels to connect with the selected audience and how to create and distribute content.

This section will offer a guide to making decisions about which social media platforms should be used for a particular campaign.

For example each platform has its content limit on the amount of textual content that can be placed in one post. For Facebook: 2,200 characters; LinkedIn: 3,000 characters; X (formerly known as Twitter): 280 characters.

Yet, this character limit might change; thus, it is necessary for digital marketing experts to stay informed.

It can be useful to keep up to date through subscriptions to platforms or agencies that update their professional users on all the changes social networks are making. Some of these may be Hubspot, Hootsuite or Metricool. In addition, most social networks have a microsite on their website dedicated to companies, which provides relevant updates and practical advice for social media managers.

The following business guides could be a useful starting point:

- www.facebook.com/business
- business.instagram.com
- www.tiktok.com/business
- www.twitch.tv/company
- business.pinterest.com

Table 4.1 provides an overview of the characteristics of some social media platforms, which should be taken into consideration while designing the campaigns.

Social Media Mix

The strategic selection of the social media channels to engage with is one of the most critical decisions for digital marketing professionals. As it can be seen from Table 4.1, some channels serve multiple functions or actions; thus, it is essential to be consistent with the decisions made. A general guideline is to think about the main target audience that should be reached (Shepherd and Lane, 2019).

Due to the many and evolving channels, social media management requires professionals who understand how each platform works and its strengths (Kalbaska and Cantoni, 2019). When a company develops its social media plan, it should consider the resources available, such as the number of employees who will work on the management of social networks, who will make the content, the kind of content that can be developed and the available tools (Nobile et al., 2021). Based on this information, the social media manager can decide which social media mix they want to carry out.

TABLE 4.1 Social media platforms' audience, use and fashion marketing activities

Platform	*Audience*	*Best use for*	*Fashion marketing activities*
Facebook	An even spread of Generation X and Millennials	Brand awareness; advertising B2B, B2C	Shares promotions, new products and company information. Resolves consumer questions. Provides direct sales space. Allows access to a wide audience of different generations, both internationally and locally. Providing traffic to the website. Promotions are often widely shared by users.
TikTok	Primarily followed by Gen Z and Millennials	Short-form, creative video content; user-generated content; brand awareness B2C	Sharing the brand universe and storytelling. Direct videos. Content and informal relationship. Close relationship with fans focused on entertainment. Close relationship with content creators. Participation in games or challenges, interaction with the community. Product release.
Instagram	Primarily Millennials	High-quality images and videos; user-generated content; advertising B2C	Sharing the brand universe and storytelling. Quality images showing products, stores, inspiration, designs, events, etc. Shows the brand's day-to-day life. Close relationship with content creators, key opinion leaders and influencers. Close relationship with users, allows us to find and promote user-generated content. Participation in contests. Shows short and direct videos. Shows direct videos about events. Participation in fashion week. Interaction of content and actions with related brands or competitors. Makes the brand's workers known. Tests products or designs to see if the community likes them. Exhibits products. Makes catalogues. Encourages promotions. Provides customer service.

(*Continued*)

TABLE 4.1 (Continued)

Platform	*Audience*	*Best use for*	*Fashion marketing activities*
X (formerly known as Twitter)	Primarily Millennials	Public relations; customer service; community building B2B and B2C	Broadcasting of company events. Participates in fashion-related social events. Shares company news, especially corporate news. Some fashion brands also use it as a customer service channel.
LinkedIn	Baby Boomers, Generation X and Millennials	B2B relationships, business development and social selling	Shares company news, especially corporate news; search and selection of talent for companies. Transmits corporate branding actions.
YouTube	Primarily Millennials but has a strong audience across gender and age demographics	Brand awareness; long-form entertainment, and how-to videos B2C and B2B	Transmission of events. Shares medium and long campaign videos. Shares summary videos of events. Shares how-to videos, especially in those products that require knowledge of use, such as makeup and beauty products. Shares fashion films.
Pinterest	Primarily Millennials with a solid audience in Gen Z, Gen X and Baby Boomers	Visual advertising; inspiration B2C	Inspiration. Generates web traffic. Shows product catalogue with direct links. Shows brand universe with content generated by other users.
WhatsApp	All, Gen Z, Millennials, Gen X and Baby Boomers	Business relationships; customer service B2C, B2B	Provides customer support. Conducts direct sale.

Source: Adaptation by the authors to the fashion industry from *Social Media Marketing: The Ultimate Guide* (2022)

Based on what has been explained, we can define the social media mix as the combination of actions on different social platforms to reach consumers and achieve our objectives delineated in the social media marketing plan. The social media mix, presented in Figure 4.1, will have to take into account three aspects: through which social media platform the content is going to be disseminated (social media platform), who is going create the content (content production) and if the content will be created by the brand itself or by a third party and if it will be free or paid (content distribution).

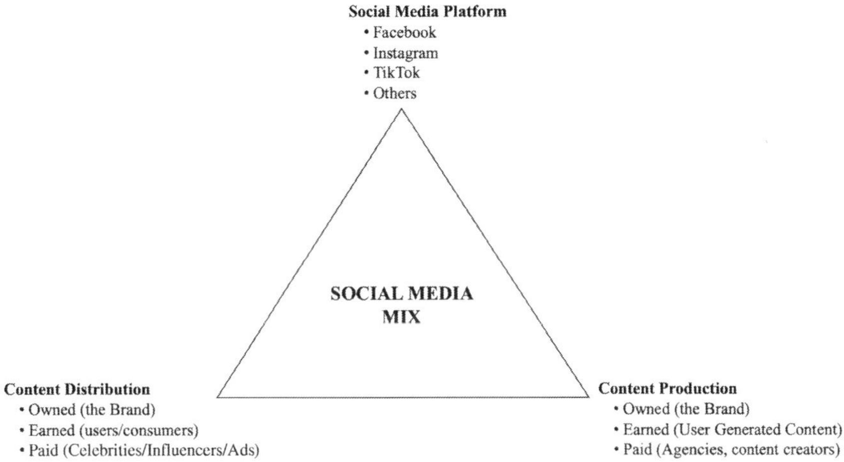

FIGURE 4.1 Social media mix

TABLE 4.2 Types of social media content and possible distribution

Owned	Content shared through the brand's social networks. Created and designed by the brand itself.
Earned	Any account or profile on social networks that freely share the content of the brand. eWOM, for example, users who share posts and videos. Fashion magazines that want to keep their community informed about something related to the brand. Influencers who like the content and share it for free.
Paid	Any content that is paid for its distribution, for example ads in the platforms. Influencers that share paid brand content in their social network profiles. Social networks of fashion magazines. Payment ambassadors or affiliates. Mass media through the social networks.

Table 4.2 shows the elaborated options available for the distribution and development of the content on social media.

The social media mix does not have to be static; yet, some consistency should be reached in order to evaluate and measure results and develop a coherent strategy that is perceived as such by the consumer.

Finally, it is essential to educate followers by telling them—explicitly or implicitly—what they can find in each social network of the brand, when videos are published, who the community is, where users' content is shared and when live videos are broadcast. With order and education, it is easier to get social network users to repeat their behaviour and create community and brand loyalty.

Note

1 Application Programming Interface (API) is a platform provided by the social networks allowing other applications and websites to pull the social media data and integrate with their site or application.

Bibliography

Hubspot, 2021. *Social media marketing: The ultimate guide*. Hubspot, 19 October. Available at: https://blog.hubspot.com/marketing/social-media-marketing. (Accessed: 13 December 2023).

Kalbaska, N. and Cantoni, L., 2019. Digital fashion competences: Market practices and needs. In *Business models and ICT technologies for the fashion supply chain: Proceedings of IT4Fashion 2017 and IT4Fashion 2018* (pp. 125–135). Springer International Publishing.

Nobile, T.H., Kalbaska, N., de Oliveira, R.A. and Cantoni, L., 2021. Digital fashion competences: A longitudinal study. In *Fashion communication: Proceedings of the FACTUM 21 conference, Pamplona, Spain, 2021* (pp. 17–28). Springer International Publishing.

Shepherd, H. and Lane, J., 2019. In the mix: Social integration and social media adoption. *Social Science Research*, *82*, pp. 1–17.

SECTION 3

Social Media Performance

This section covers the implementation and the execution of the social media content plan, which involves the strategic development of three types of actions: Actions to improve commerce in social networks, actions to create a content plan and actions to develop a social media CRM and enhance the brand community. These topics are explained in the following chapters:

- Chapter 5, ***Social Media Commerce Strategy***, focuses on how to develop a commercial strategy in social networks. The tools or commercial facilities offered by the social platforms most used by fashion companies to sell their products are discussed here.
- Chapter 6, ***Social Media Content Strategy***, explains in detail how to develop a social media content action plan. To do so, it addresses the different objectives associated with the different types of content formats, their production and distribution. It then addresses the specific content that fashion brands can share on social networks. Finally, the chapter explains the importance of creating a content calendar and how a hashtag strategy can be developed.
- Chapter 7, ***Social Media Customer Relationship Management and Community* Strategy**, focuses on how to develop a social media CRM strategy and introduces some of the social media CRM tools that fashion brands can use. Subsequently, some key considerations for developing a brand community strategy are addressed.
- Chapter 8, ***Calendar, Budget, Monitoring and Tools***, covers actions necessary to develop a professional social media plan. It explains the importance of making a global social media calendar, not only with the contents but also with all the campaigns planned for the different collections that a fashion company carries out. It gives insights into how to manage the social media budget. Finally,

DOI: 10.4324/9781003505495-8

it explains how to monitor social media performance and needed tools for this activity.

After reading this section, you will:

- Be able to execute a professional social media plan for fashion brands
- Know that social media plans for fashion brands need to address commercial and editorial aspects
- Know how to manage the brand's users/customers through a CRM strategy
- Be exposed to several professional tools and techniques, which will make your work smooth

5

SOCIAL MEDIA COMMERCE STRATEGY

Introduction

This chapter focuses on social media commerce strategies, also known in the digital marketing field as 'social commerce.' First, it addresses the topic of social commerce strategy and its potential benefits in social networks. Then, it introduces the most valuable platforms for fashion brands in the social media business, briefly describing the tools that help brands promote and sell their products. To conclude, it presents how ad campaigns can be carried out on social networks. For this purpose, the case of Meta, which manages Facebook and Instagram platforms, is explained, as it was the most important social network for social commerce at the time during which this book was written. In addition, the learnings from the Meta example can be extrapolated to other social networks.

Social Media Commerce Strategy

The increased use of social networks and the proliferation of company accounts have resulted in social networks becoming a channel for social commerce.

Social commerce describes online retail that uses social networks or peer-to-peer communication to drive sales (WARC, 2021). Social commerce activities may be focused on influencing users at the pre-purchase, purchase or post-purchase stages (Abed et al., 2015). Through social media commerce, companies can (Singh and Diamond, 2012):

- Raise awareness of new products
- Teach customers how to care for their products
- Develop or sell new product lines in response to customer comments and reactions

DOI: 10.4324/9781003505495-9

- Adapt their business to match customer needs
- Promote seasonal bargains and marketing messages

A recent (WARC (2021) report prepared in collaboration with TikTok and Publicis Groupe explores the role that social communities play in influencing purchasing decisions through social networks.

Four key points were highlighted:

- Community commerce, as an emerging opportunity, sits at the intersection of community, shopping and entertainment which is growing, driven by the adoption of digital technologies in our daily lives. With the right approach, brands can fit seamlessly into the social media experience, and those who are willing to test and learn are already reaping the rewards.
- Discovery and inspiration disrupt the path to purchase. Social media has disrupted the purchase journey, which is now led by spontaneous discovery and inspiration. Every moment on a platform is an opportunity for conversion, and authentic creativity is key to attracting and retaining the audience's attention.
- Propelling purchase decisions. To maximise opportunities, brands must make the most of technologies that facilitate a seamless community commerce experience. All product categories can potentially convert audiences: Beauty, clothing and accessories led the way, and now luxury and automotive are also maximising opportunities.
- New ways to tell brand stories. Community is a powerful force of social commerce. Social media platforms provide a space where creators and brands can build high levels of engagement that drive inspiration and purchase. Creators boost discovery, motivate audiences to try new products and help make a brand relatable.

To capitalise on social commerce, brands are advised to (WARC, 2021):

- Create better mobile social commerce experiences, especially on mobile-specific social media platforms
- Become more visually driven, relatable and authentic so that the content can stand out from fast-rolling mobile news feeds
- Build trust and consumer confidence with online experiences that demonstrate clear value—and security—of browsing and shopping via social channels.
- Test and measure the effectiveness of any investment
- Constantly optimise the evolving customer journey to reflect on online behaviour

Therefore, in order to carry out correct social commerce strategies, it is essential to know users' behaviour on each of the social networks, their buying process and the products that are best sold on each social network. We should not forget that 'social commerce isn't just about making a feed shoppable; it is also about providing thumb-stopping content that engages, delights and inspires consumers' (Bain, 2021).

As in almost all digital communication channels, paid marketing actions can also be carried out on social networks. Brands can pay to reach new audiences to whom they want to show their content. Most of these actions have commercial purposes, known as paid media or social media ads.

Social Media Business Tools and Commerce Facilities

Brands, driven by the possible positive effects of social media, have been gradually monetising their social communities not only by giving the possibility of creating ads—as seen earlier—but also by creating specific spaces for the sale of products and services.

The facilities and tools provided by social networks for the dissemination and marketing of products are constantly evolving and adapting to the new e-commerce platforms. For this reason, social networks usually enable spaces on their websites dedicated to 'Business' (e.g. Facebook Business or TikTok Business, where they update all the changes and give tips to brands). This section focuses on the social networks most used by marketing and communication professionals from fashion companies to promote and sell their products. The most important sales and dissemination tools of each platform are explained next, along with a word-by-word description of the features of the platforms.

Facebook[1]

- Checkout: Let customers buy items directly from your shop on Facebook
- Live shopping: Sell products, interact with viewers and reach new customers in live video. Facebook Live Shopping is an interactive way to sell items, connect directly with your audience and reach potential customers, all in real time. When you sell products using Facebook's Live Shopping feature, you broadcast live while showing your products and demonstrating how they are used
- Product tagging: Let people start shopping directly through your posts. You can tag products from your Facebook Page catalogue or store them in photos and videos. When people see the tagged products in your posts, they can select those tags to start shopping
- Shops: Let people browse and purchase your products on Facebook and Instagram. A store is your online storefront where people can browse, discover and purchase your products directly on Facebook and Instagram. With customisable collections and simple design tools, you can showcase featured products, bring your brand to life and make shopping for your products a seamless experience for your customers

Instagram[2]

- Stores: Customisable storefronts that allow you to shop directly from company profiles
- Shopping tags: These are tags that include the products in your catalogue and direct customers to your website or app to purchase them
- Store in the 'Explore' section: A tab from which you can explore content from brands and creators with tagged products

- Collections: Sets of products that companies can create in their stores to make it easy for customers to find products they like
- Product detail page: A page that displays the most important information about a product, such as price or description, which is pulled directly from your catalogue
- Ads with product tags: Businesses can create new ads with product tags or promote existing shopping posts in Instagram's ad manager and app to increase their reach. These ads increase conversions, link clicks and engagement with the post
- Product releases: This solution allows product releases to be announced on Instagram so that details can be viewed in advance and reminders can be set up to purchase a product as soon as it becomes available
- Permissions for shopping partners: A set of permissions that companies can grant to partners on Instagram to increase the product reach. A shopping partner is an account that gives or receives permission to tag products or link a store to another account
- Live shopping: Businesses and creators can tag products when live-streaming on Instagram. This type of shopping allows businesses to share products with their audiences

TikTok[3]

- In-Feed Ads: video format that integrates seamlessly with user-generated content appearing in the personalised 'For You' feed
- In-Feed One Day Max: The first ad users see on your For You page with an In-Feed One Day Max, typically positioned after the first three organic TikToks
- TopView; Captures the attention of all TikTok users the moment they open the app by taking over their entire screen. The TopView video format guarantees millions of views in just 24 hours and achieves fantastic brand awareness and engagement results
- TopView Lite: like TopView, this is the first thing users see when they open the app. This soundless format captures attention in just five seconds
- Branded Hashtag Challenge: Launch challenges and start viral movements; this is the most popular format, and let TikTok's creative community respond to your challenge by creating and sharing their own videos
- Branded Hashtag Challenge PLUS: The same visibility as the Branded Hashtag Challenge but with an integrated shopping element to increase your sales without leaving TikTok
- Branded Effects: Generate brand awareness and engagement on a large scale with branded effects and create unforgettable moments for users
- Creator Marketplace: Through our Creator Marketplace, you can access over 1,000 incredibly talented users to help you launch your campaigns

Pinterest[4]

- Catalogue: Turn your entire catalogue into Product Pins that can be browsed at the same time. Once you upload a catalogue, a shopping tab appears on your profile, making it easy for shoppers to find your products. You can even upload multiple feeds to the same account to control which products are displayed on different marketplaces
- Tags: Add the Pinterest tag to your site in order to measure conversions and optimise ads for shopping campaigns or retargeting. Consider using wider referral windows to capture shoppers who take longer to convert
- Shopify-Connected Store: Connect your Pinterest business account from the Shopify app. From there, they will automatically add your catalogue to Pinterest, set up your Pinterest tag and add a shopping tab to your Pinterest profile. Your entire catalogue can be browsed with just a few click
- Shopping Ads: Reach shoppers at the right time. Shopping ads include useful details such as pricing, product availability and reviews
- Collections Ads: This immersive format uses slideshows and video content to help users buy similar products. They are great for generating larger sales because they help shoppers find more products they like
- Automatic Ads: With automatic bids, Pinterest will dynamically adjust bids over time to deliver the maximum amount of conversions possible for your budget. With campaign budgets, setup is simpler than ever, and you'll get more results more efficiently

Social Media Advertising: Meta Case

The Meta case is presented to show the steps that can be followed to carry out an advertising campaign on Facebook or Instagram. These social networks have been selected as they bring together the most advertising budget spent on social networks by fashion companies.[5]

First of all, fashion brands must select and define through the business platform of the social network the audience for ads campaign and the objective. Once the audience and objectives are determined, the brand must choose between three types of strategies: Prospecting, remarketing and up-cross selling. Each step is explained next:[6]

1) Select the audience for ads campaign.

- *Basic Audiences:* Define an audience based on certain criteria, such as age, interests, geographic region and more
- *Custom Audiences*: Reconnect with people who have interacted with your business, both online and offline
- *Similar Audiences:* Reach new people with interests similar to those of your best customers

2) Define the audience. The tool offers five characteristics of the users of the social network through which the target is defined:

   - *Location:* Advertise in cities, communities and countries where you are interested in doing business
   - *Demographics:* Choose an audience based on their age, gender, educational background, job title and more. While you can track the types of people you reach with your ads, Facebook will never share personally identifiable information about them
   - *Interests:* Add the interests and hobbies of the people you want your ad to reach, from organic food to action movies, and bring relevance to targeted ads
   - *Behaviour:* Display your ads based on consumer behaviour, such as past purchases and device usage
   - *Connections:* Include people connected to your Facebook Page or event, or exclude them from finding new audiences

3) Select objectives. The tool allows one to select between 11 objectives grouped in the phases attention, consideration and conversion. Generally, Meta platform recommends two objectives per campaign

   - Attention objectives:
     - *Brand recognition:* Show ads to those most likely to pay attention to them to increase your overall brand recognition
     - *Reach*: Show ads to the maximum number of people in your audience without exceeding your budget. You can also choose to reach only those who are close to your business locations
   - Consideration objectives:
     - *Traffic:* Increase the number of people who visit your website, access your app or have a Messenger conversation with your company and increase the likelihood that they will take valuable action when they reach their destination
     - *Lead generation:* Make it easier for interested people to learn more about your company. Encourage them to sign up for that information or invest time in your app or website
     - *Messaging:* Encourage people to initiate more interactions on Messenger. Expand your ability to have personal conversations with them so you can answer questions, collect information from potential customers and drive sales
     - *Interaction:* Get more people to follow your page or interact with your posts by leaving comments, sharing content or liking them. You can also choose to optimise your advertising in order to get more responses to events or requests for offers
     - *Video views:* Show your videos to the people most likely to be interested in them and watch them to the end

    - *App downloads:* Link directly to the App Store and Google Play Store to increase your app downloads. You can also choose to target high-value users
- Conversion objectives:
    - *Conversions:* Increase the actions that take place on your website or app. Whether you are interested in getting purchases, leads, registrations or other types of conversions, this goal will encourage people to take action
    - *In-store visits:* Combine online and offline shopping journeys to increase in-store visits, sales and other valuable actions in your stores
    - *Catalogue sales:* Automatically promote the most relevant products to sell more of your inventory. Just upload the catalogue and set up the campaign, which will show the right products to the right people

Once the audience and objectives are determined, the brand must choose between three types of strategies for the paid campaigns on social networks: Prospecting, remarketing and up-cross selling. Table 5.1 shows the types of campaigns that can be performed on Facebook to reach desired audiences.

TABLE 5.1 Strategies for campaigns on social networks

Prospecting	*Remarketing*	*Up-cross selling*
Display advertising to identify potential customers who are likely to engage with your brand. These campaigns are useful for generating new traffic. The marketer has to select which audience to target (Basic/Custom/Similar) and define the audience through the variables offered by Facebook (location, demographics, interests, etc.). Once the audience is selected, the objective of the prospecting campaign will be set (capture attention or generate consideration).	It consists of implementing the Facebook tracking code on a web page (this code is a pixel or SDK—Software Development Kit). In this way, you can keep track of people who visited a web page, viewed products and even added them to the cart so that you can later show them those products again on Facebook and remind them that they were interested in that product. Example: A consumer enters Nike's website and is interested in running shoes but finally does not buy them. Subsequently, through a campaign, the brand can show him those running shoes again in a Facebook ad.	Upsell: For a consumer who is considering one product, the campaigns offer to switch to another product that would have higher profitability. Example: If the consumer is going to buy an umbrella worth 10€, an ad is displayed proposing to buy a better umbrella for 20€. Cross-sell: If a consumer buys an item that is part of a set of products. This option is useful for increasing a customer's total value. For the users with completed conversion, new products are proposed. Example: If the consumer is going to buy a pair of wellies, an ad is shown that also proposes buying an umbrella or a raincoat.

Source: Own elaboration

Notes

1 https://es-es.facebook.com/business
2 https://www.facebook.com/business/
3 https://www.tiktok.com/business
4 https://business.pinterest.com/es/shopping/
5 https://www.statista.com/statistics/1295282/miv-fashion-luxury-brands-usa/; https://www.statista.com/statistics/1254990/united-states-leading-social-networks-apparel-fashion-shopping/
6 https://www.facebook.com/business/ads/ad-targeting; https://www.facebook.com/business/ads/ad-objectives

Bibliography

Abed, S.S., Dwivedi, Y.K. and Williams, M.D., 2015. Social media as a bridge to e-commerce adoption in SMEs: A systematic literature review. *The Marketing Review*, *15*(1), pp. 39–57.

Bain, M., 2021. *Future gazing: Social commerce is the new e-commerce*. WARC. Available at: https://www.warc.com/content/paywall/article/warc-exclusive/future-gazing-social-commerce-is-the-new-e-commerce/en-gb/135733 (Accessed: 12 December 2023).

Singh, S. and Diamond, S., 2012. *Social media marketing for dummies* (pp. 1–432). John Wiley & Sons.

WARC, 2021. *From discovery to purchase: The role of community commerce*. WARC. Available at: https://www.warc.com/content/paywall/article/warc-exclusive/from-discovery-to-purchase-the-role-of-community-commerce/en-gb/139665 (Accessed: 12 December 2023).

6

SOCIAL MEDIA CONTENT STRATEGY

Introduction

This chapter explains how to carry out a content strategy on social networks. It is important to remember that social networks are digital platforms through which content is shared; thus, it is possible to say that content is the centrepiece through which relationships and user interactions revolve.

The chapter begins with the definition of content marketing. Second, it explains the specific objectives of content creation and possible formats. Subsequently, it explains the various ways that can be adopted to create and distribute content, and it presents the different types of content that fashion brands can create for distribution on social networks. Potential communication crises that can occur on social media are also introduced. Finally, the creation of a content calendar and hashtag strategy are discussed.

Social Media Content Marketing

Content marketing is defined as a 'strategic marketing approach focused on creating and distributing valuable, relevant and consistent content to attract and retain a clearly defined audience—and, ultimately, to drive profitable customer action' (Content Marketing Institute, 2022). Content marketing can also be defined 'as creation of content for creating awareness by attracting the target audience and beyond to the firm, making products and services appealing, reaching the target audience, establishing a relationship with them, and acquiring measurable results by mobilising them' (Gümüş, 2017, p. 2). For this reason, social media content marketing plays an important role in communicating effective content to consumers, making it alluring for consumers to stay connected with brands (Gümüş, 2017).

DOI: 10.4324/9781003505495-10

As explained in the chapter on strategy in relation to the maturity levels of social media strategies, brands should develop their social content strategy, given that content popularity and vitality are influenced by social message strategy, seeding strategy and context, product characteristics, organisational processes and IT tools.

In order to carry out a successful content strategy, a brand must develop its editorial plan. The editorial plan is the execution of the content plan, which specifies what kind of content will be created, when the content will be published and how it will be published. Therefore, in order to carry out the editorial plan, it is important to:

1. Find relevant topics, focus the content on meeting the audience's needs and create a story around desirable qualities and unique value propositions that only the brand can provide. The selection of topics is a consequence of the strategic brand concept explained in the previous chapter of the book
2. Use a content calendar to organise brand messages and prepare the hashtag strategy
3. Publishing guidelines: Defines characteristics of the brand identity, including preferred editorial style details and the tone of voice

Content Objectives and Formats

The digital platform Smartinsights categorises the types of content into four groups according to their objectives: Entertain, inspire, educate and convince.

- Entertain: Games, competitions, quizzes, virals, mobile apps, etc.
- Inspire: Endorsements, testimonials, forum comments, reviews, etc.
- Educate: Articles, guides, infographics, reports, press releases, etc.
- Convince: Features of the product, checklists, ratings, financial aid calculations

In social networks, the type of content is limited to the content formats that the platforms allow sharing through their application. These formats change very frequently, so an important task of social media professionals is to keep up to date with the topics and formats which are allowed by the platforms they decide to use.

Examples of formats are:

- Facebook: Videos, blog posts, curated content
- Twitter: Industry news, blog posts, tweets on general news/trending topics
- LinkedIn: Job listings, webinars, blog posts, interviews, content about the company and work culture
- Instagram: Stories and images of employees, ad campaigns, events, behind the scenes
- YouTube: Interviews, in-depth videos, top-shots, informative motion graphics

For fashion brands, it is essential to create *brand content*. This content must be of quality, follow the storytelling, recreate the brand's universe, transmit the brand values and its attributes, be inspirational and provide value.

A further concept related to social media content strategy is content curation. *Content curation* is the grouping of digital content to maintain, preserve and add value. In this regard, it is important that social media content curators consider the journey on which they take their audience with the content they select and the way in which they present it (Sutherland, 2021).

In the content curation process, the curator has to make sure that the content does not present any legal, copyright or ethical problems and also has to be sure of the quality of the content from the audience's perspective. For this purpose, the curator analyses four variables related to the content (Handley and Chapman, 2010, p. 7):

- Interesting: How interesting will this content be for the audience?
- Relevant: Does the content align with the audience's day-to-day lives?
- Valuable: How helpful will this content be for your audience? Does it help to solve a common problem or challenge?
- Credible. Is the content accurate and was taken from a credible source?

Content Creation and Distribution

The *social media content mix* is a combination of content created by the brand, content created by consumers and content created by those whom the brands pay, such as influencers. Therefore, the content mix will have to have a combination according to the objectives of the brand and the moment of maturity in which it finds itself. As it can be observed in Table 6.1, content production is related to the social media mix.

Fashion Content and Activities in Social Media

As we have seen in the introduction of this book, communication plays an essential role in fashion as all the elements of the company are communicative elements: The brand, the company's history, events, stores, production processes, fashion archives as a source of inspiration for the designers, etc.

Below, we explain some of the most relevant actions that occur in a fashion company that can be communicated through social networks and other specific actions that take place on social networks.

- ***Fashion Shows***

Throughout history, fashion shows have been the most important communication event for haute couture houses. A fashion show is an event with great media appeal due to the designs, colours and new trends proposed by the designers of each brand,

TABLE 6.1 Advantages and disadvantages of content production

How to produce content	*Advantages*	*Disadvantages*	*Fashion content example*
OWNED ***Company-Generated Content***	—The brand is in control of the message and when it wants to be broadcast. —The brand controls 100% of its production.	The company can only disseminate it through its channels.	—Informative videos and photos about the brand. —Product photos and videos. —Events streams. —Videos on how products are produced.
EARNED ***User-Generated Content***	—Content that the users generate for free and share on their channels; the company can also share it without incurring production costs. —It is organic content that usually generates good interaction in the consumer's community and is perceived as highly trusted by other consumers.	The brand cannot exercise control over the message or its production.	—Videos and photos that users take with the products they buy on a daily basis. —Product and brand reviews.
PAID ***Influencer-Generated Content***	—The company has control of the message and when it wants to be disseminated. —Influencers share the content created on their social networks, amplifying the brand's ability to reach new users.	Influencers and creators want to have freedom of creation, so they limit the control of the brand.	—Inspirational videos and photos. —Product usage and feedback.

Source: Own elaboration

as well as guests invited to the fashion shows, especially the personalities that make up the front row.

In recent years, broadcasting fashion shows through social networks has become an essential element. Many fashion brands decide to broadcast it live through social platforms and encourage the involvement of models, celebrities and attendees in disseminating the parade. Many brand ambassadors or influencers also broadcast through social networks how they prepare for the event, show how they received the invitation and what look they will wear. Brands also often prepare a red carpet before the fashion show, where the media take photos of the attendees, and many of them are interviewed to gather their opinions.

For all these events, it is essential to prepare #hashtags that allow network users to follow the event and all the content published.

The activation of social networks during fashion shows produces an Impact Media Value (IMV) of great importance for fashion companies. Currently, there is software that allows monitoring social networks, mentions and measures IMV, such as Launchmetrics.

- ***Presentation of Collections***

Haute couture and ready-to-wear brands often present their collections at fashion shows, but many fashion brands, especially small and medium-sized companies or fast-fashion chains, present their collections through events, press releases and social media. To do so, they create lookbooks, photos and videos that they disseminate through social networks. These contents are usually associated with a #hashtag, with the main theme of the collection, and another of the collection, for example, #SSS, #FW.

- ***Shootings***

These are photo shoots where the new collections of the brands are photographed with professional models. These photoshoots were first made for the lookbooks of the brands, but with the advent of e-commerce, photos of models and products are constantly made to make the cards and online sales pages. Shootings are also made for the realisation of editorial content, both for fashion magazines and for the websites of the brands. More and more fashion brands take advantage of these moments to share content (photos and videos) on social networks about the process, as well as share the results of the shootings.

- ***Opening***

As fashion companies grow, they open new stores in many locations. Store openings are a special occasion to hold an event party and raise awareness of the brand and the new store. Celebrities, models, journalists and influencers are often invited to these openings. These events are also communicated through social media before, during and after. Hashtags are often made to publicise the event so social media users can follow the events. Brands ensure that all these events have a great visual appeal to encourage being photographed or recorded by attendees.

- ***Collaborations with Models***

Brands collaborate with models who are invited to participate in fashion shows, lookbooks or shootings and are often encouraged to share some photos on their social networks. It is advisable that those responsible for digital communication coordinate with the professionals who deal with the models.

- ***Collaborations with Brand Representatives/Brand Ambassadors***

Brands collaborate with ambassadors or brand representatives, who are key pieces in the communication of fashion companies. They participate in fashion shows, openings, ad campaigns and events. These ambassadors must have a good relationship with the brand and feel a great attraction to it. In this way, the generation of organic content is supported naturally. Sometimes, brands generate special hashtags with the name of the brand and the influencer for social networks.

- ***ePR***

All fashion brands must carry out a strong public relations activity through social networks. The most effective way is to have a public relations manager or director. In this way, they can have more informal contact with models and representatives, constantly interact with the content shared, learn about their daily lives and often forge friendships with them.

- ***Influencer Marketing***

Influencers have communities of followers among whom they disseminate both organic content and paid collaborations. In their day-to-day lives, they share their looks, give fashion advice and broadcast events they attend. As mentioned earlier, fashion brands can collaborate with them both in content creation and in content broadcasting. More and more brands are implementing influencer marketing strategies through social networks with the aim of reaching new audiences or having their products presented by these opinion leaders, bringing confidence to consumers.

- ***Digital Storefronts***

Social media profiles, especially Instagram or Pinterest, function as a showcase for the brand. Fashion brands must constantly update their content to be in line with the collections or new designs that are presented both in stores and on the website.

- ***Promotion: Coupons, Discounts, Special Offers***

Much of the information shared by fashion brands is related to the dissemination of promotions on their products. Brands can communicate sale periods and special discounts or offer promotions to their followers to encourage participation in social networks.

- ***Contests***

Through social networks, many fashion brands hold contests with the aim of encouraging community interaction and gaining new followers. These may consist of sharing photos or videos, making comments, mentioning users on social networks or creating specific content. The prizes of these contests can be branded fashion products, discounts or trips. Sometimes, contests are held in collaboration with influencers to activate interaction with the brand in the influencer's community of followers.

- ***Limited Editions***

Fashion brands can make limited editions that they advertise through social networks or collections that are only sold online. These collections are usually announced through social networks where the creative process of the collection is also a source of storytelling. Some fashion brands are making collections with influencers in order to make their products go viral and encourage sales among their followers.

- ***Avatars***

There are more and more avatars or digital models that have large communities of followers on social networks. Many fashion brands collaborate with them in order to publicise their products or invite them to participate in digital events. With the arrival of the Metaverse, more and more brands will be interacting with avatars on social networks or creating their own avatars to promote their products through these new channels.

- ***Fashion Press***

Fashion and lifestyle magazines have profiles on all social networks. Through these communication channels, they spread their content and interact with readers, brands and celebrities. They often share content where they mention fashion brands, and these, in turn, spread it among their communities. Social networks are a communication platform between brands, fashion professionals and journalists.

Moreover, fashion brands can also share more industry and business-focused information about the company through social media. This type of information is mainly disseminated through social networks such as LinkedIn or X (formerly known as Twitter). Such information is also sometimes shared by the channels of various portals such as The Business of Fashion or Vogue Business.

Possible Communication Crisis on Social Media

Despite their multiple potential benefits, social media professionals must also be prepared to face possible communication crises on social media channels. In several cases, fashion brands have misstepped while managing their social media campaigns and profiles (Noris and Cantoni, 2022).

The Fashion Business Manual (2018, pp. 128–129) presents a list of 12 elements that fashion companies can communicate in order to prevent a possible communication crisis:

1. Company direction: Share the current standpoint and future direction of your company
2. Product development: Communicate new product developments to keep loyal customers excited and engaged
3. Materials' sourcing: Showcase where and how your materials are sourced
4. Supply chain: Be open about your company's factory and its working conditions, especially if you have highlighted your brand's own social responsibility. A virtual tour of the factory on your website is the perfect way to do this
5. Staff spotlight: Profile team members and factory workers to highlight staff dedication and company values
6. Inventory level: Display real-time stock levels to show transparency and create a sense of urgency to purchase when stock is low. This will entice shoppers to buy more quickly in fear of missing out
7. Product production: Highlight the process of how your products are created
8. Behind-the-scenes footage: Share never-seen-before photos or videos that capture unofficial moments from photo shoots or events
9. Event updates: Share event preparations and post-event celebrations to help customers feel connected to your brand

10. Customer feedback: Allow customers to comment through a public review or rating system, which is also useful to other potential customers
11. Team building activities: Let customers see your staff working or socialising together to reinforce your company's team values
12. Company progression: Share your company's growth and expansion by offering updates such as an office relocation or the opening of a new retail space

Content Calendar

As we have seen already throughout this book, managing social media is a challenging activity, as there are many elements that have to be taken into consideration regarding the consumers to reach, social platforms to use and the content to publish. Being consistent and offering a good experience to the consumer through social networks is the result of the coordination and supervision of the entire team working with these channels.

Therefore, it is essential to work with a content calendar that allows to organise all the activities on social networks efficiently and in advance. As Hubspot mentions, a social media content calendar is a planner for businesses to schedule the content for their posts, the publication time and the platforms on which the content will be published. The recommended content that this type of calendar has to offer is:

- Content types
- Post title
- Link for the content
- Text
- Image link
- Publication date and time

Content calendars in fashion companies are complicated as fashion brands work with a very challenging production and sales calendar due to the high number of collections they produce each year, especially if we are talking about fast-fashion brands.

In the same month, many events take place. For example, in Europe in January, there is a sales period, and at the same time the brands have already introduced many garments in store from the new spring or cruise collections. Additionally, the buying teams (on the production side) are developing the future fall/winter collection, and the design teams are working on the spring/summer collection for the following year. Hence, it is essential to develop a good strategy for each social network and decide what content to publish on each social network and when to publish it.

That's not all, as a large number of holidays and promotional days must also be taken into account, for example, by delivering special content or an exclusive campaign on social networks. Some of these days are presented in Table 6.2.

TABLE 6.2 Example of social media content calendar events

January	**February**	**March**	**April**
1st New Year Fall End of Season Sales (whole month) Chinese New Year Blue Monday Paris Fashion Week Men's Fashion Haute Couture Fashion Show	Chinese New Year 14th Valentine's Day Fall end of Season Sales Grammy Awards New York Fashion Week London Fashion Week Milan Fashion Week	14th White Day (Asian Countries) 8th International Women's Rights Day 18th World Recycling Day	Easter 22th World Earth Day 23th World Book Day
May	**June**	**July**	**August**
1st Labour day Mother's Day	Summer End of Sales Season	Haute Couture Fashion Show	Back to School (Some Countries)
September	**October**	**November**	**December**
Fashion Month Presentation Fall Collections	1st to 7th Golden Week China 2nd Monday Canadian Thanksgiving 31st Halloween	11th Singles' Day 4th Thursday American Thanksgiving Black Friday Cyber Monday	25th Christmas Day 26th Boxing Day

Source: Own elaboration

Every country has national days and specific celebrations (e.g. Swiss National Day is on August 1st or Spanish one is on October 12th). So, if the companies want to be present in some specific markets, they should also take into consideration country-relevant festivities.

Hashtags Content Strategy

The main function of hashtags is to aggregate and categorise content and to help users discover it. Hashtags are beneficial to reach new audiences.

One can add them in the post's description or a comment. They can also be added to audiovisual content such as videos or stories.

Using between two and five hashtags per post is advisable to ensure they interest the audience. Social media professionals must be updated with trending social network topics. Brands in social networks must carry out a correct hashtag strategy to be consistent, make content go viral and reach the relevant audience (Karamalak et al., 2021).

The following hashtags can be defined when designing content:

- Generic fashion hashtags: #fashion, #fashionblogger, #fashionstyle, #fashionblog, #fashiongram, #fashionable, #fashionphotography, #fashionlover, #fashionaddict, #style, #styleinspo, #styleblogger, #styleinspiration, #stylegram, #styleblog, #styleoftheday, #fashioninspo, #fashioninsta, #fashiondesign, #outfitoftheday,

#fashionweek, #fashionaddict, #fashionistas, #fashionstyle, #fashionable, #fashionista, #style, #beautiful, #beauty, #makeupoftheday, #makeupfanatic, #wakeupandmakeu

- Hasgtags most popular for a social network (Instagram example): #love, #instagood, #photooftheday, #fashion, #beautiful, #happy, #cute, #tbt, #like4like, #followme, #picoftheday, #follow, #me, #selfie, #summer, #art, #instadaily, #friends, #repost, #nature, #girl, #fun, #style, #smile, #food
- Trending topic hashtags: #BlackLivesMatter
- Product hashtags: #denim, #coat, #swimwear, #accessories
- Fashion brand hashtags: #nike, #dior, #mango
- Campaign hashtags: Can be associated with the season—#springsummer, #cruise, #christmas, #halloween, or associated with the theme (storytelling or slogan) of the campaign

It is also important to determine the prohibited hashtags for a campaign—for example those that do not represent the brand's values or may be socially sensitive due to their impact and might eventually cause a communication crisis. Some examples of sensitive social trends hashtags can be #curvygirls, #bikinibody, #underwear and #undies. Using prohibited hashtags can lead to a drop in reach and interactions; thus, they should be selected carefully.

Bibliography

Content Marketing Institute, 2022. *What is content marketing?* Content Marketing Institute. Available at: https://contentmarketinginstitute.com/what-is-content-marketing/ (Accessed: 10 June 2022).

Fashionary, 2021. The Fashion Business Manual. An illustrated guide to building a fashion brand. Fashionary International Ltd.

Gümüş, N., 2017. The effects of social media content marketing activities of firms on consumers' brand following behavior. *Academic Research International*, *8*(1), pp. 1–8.

Handley, A. and Chapman, C.C., 2010. *Content rules: How to create killer blogs, podcasts, videos, ebooks, webinars (and more) that engage customers and ignite your business* (Vol. 5). John Wiley & Sons.

Hubspot, 2021. *Social media content calendar*. Hubspot. Available at: https://offers.hubspot.com/social-media-content-calendar (Accessed: 25 June 2022).

Karamalak, O., Kalbaska, N. and Cantoni, L., 2021. What do hashtags afford in digital fashion communication? An exploratory study on Gucci-related hashtags on Twitter and Instagram. *Semiotica*, *2021*(243), pp. 325–351.

Noris, A. and Cantoni, L., 2022. Digital fashion communication: An (inter)cultural perspective. In *Digital fashion communication* (pp. 1–147). Brill.

Sutherland, K.E., 2020. *Strategic social media management: Theory and practice*. Springer Nature.

7

SOCIAL MEDIA CUSTOMER RELATIONSHIP MANAGEMENT AND COMMUNITY STRATEGY

Introduction

This chapter explains how to develop a customer relationship management (CRM) strategy on social networks to nurture and grow social communities. Once the content plan has been completed, brands must develop their social media CRM strategy with the aim of boosting customer engagement. Once the company is able to manage the CRM appropriately, it can develop a quality Social Media Community strategy focused on customer loyalty and brand advocacy. We will also deep dive into the activities needed to develop and manage communities on social networks.

Social Media CRM Strategy and Tools

Consumers today use multiple channels to get in touch with fashion brands. It is essential that companies develop strategies for customer service in a global and unified way because, although the contact may occur through various channels, the consumer expects from the brand a relationship such as that of face-to-face interactions. Therefore, fashion brands must establish Social Media CRM through an integrated customer service process.

We define social media CRM as the brand's process of managing customer-to-customer social media conversations to engage the existing customers and prospects. The social media company Hootsuite (2021) highlights that this strategy involves connecting social media channels with the brand CRM system to give all team members within the company a complete record of interactions with the customer or prospect. This allows better linking of customer interactions on social networks to marketing results such as purchases or subscriptions.

DOI: 10.4324/9781003505495-11

The benefits of using a social CRM system are the following (Cerchia, 2016, p. 789):

- The organisation obtains a complete image of the sales opportunities and client interactions
- Automatization of the sales processes considerably optimises operating procedures, increasing the time assigned for the sales
- The services for clients are better managed as organisations can efficiently solve the clients' requests by accessing complete databases with complaints and involved customers
- Companies can plan, implement and evaluate marketing campaigns. The marketing campaigns, activities, tasks and marketing budgets can be planned and followed up for each activity.
- The communication becomes more relevant for each segment of clients by capturing the preferences, relations and dynamic communication on social networks.
- The information is accessible worldwide, no matter the time, by each employee.

To carry out a Social Media CRM strategy, the brand has to take into account three activities:

- Social Integration: The first thing is that the fashion brands must use a tool to have all social networks connected with the sales channels. Some of these tools will be recommended later.
- Personal Relationship Perspective: Social media CRM is not a platform to promote commercial content. It is an opportunity to respond to the demands of each user or consumer. It is preferable to work on personal relationships and send direct messages than to invade the consumer with advertising.
- Social Listening: To carry out professional social media CRM strategies, companies must dedicate time and resources to social listening and detecting keywords and conversations.

Social media CRM mainly measures four variables:

1. Traffic: Social networks drive traffic from their platforms towards brand pages and e-commerce sites. Many social CRMs let brands monitor traffic and click-throughs in real time to assess how much ends up as successful sales conversions.
2. Engagement: Allows social media managers to identify all the interactions that followers have with the content that brands share on social networks, such as likes, shares, reposts, comments and incoming communications.

3. Followers: Allow better understanding of the followers, who they are, who they are connected with and how active they are online.
4. Brand mentions: Identify and coordinate all the conversations and online buzz around a brand.

To this end, it is recommended that each brand create a *customer service manual* through social networks, which explains how to interact with the community. Possible points to consider are given next:

- Always speak to your users with respect
- Give the customer the reason first and then explain the necessary issues to understand the brand's point of view in relation to a problem
- Give likes to all positive customer comments
- Answer negative comments from customers about celebrities and brand friends
- Respond closely to product questions so as not to lose potential sales
- Make sure that the customer is satisfied with the resolution of the problem and does not need further help

When selecting a tool to manage Social Media CRM, it is convenient to pay attention to the services that these tools offer (Scheiner, 2023):

- Management consumer profiles. They support a better understanding of the customer needs and issues and support faster customer service
- Social listening. As we have explained earlier, it is essential to keep track of the conversations in which the brand's followers or potential audience participate and the conversations in which the brand is involved
- Social media management. Fashion brands have many social network profiles; hence, having a platform that combines the overview of all the channels will allow the brand to offer its users a coherent social media experience
- Sentiment analysis. Some tools allow an overview of users' feelings (or even sentiments) towards the brand, its products and services and its position.
- Social selling. Knowing customers' tastes and needs allows brands to offer products in a personalised way and respond to different needs

Social Media Community Strategy

For fashion brands, the creation and management of a community of followers and brand lovers are keys to develop and maintain relationships with customers in both the short and long terms.

Social Media Community strategies are usually focused on sharing, socialising and interacting with social network users in a meaningful way, while building up a community of them.

As we mentioned at the beginning of the book, social networks have socialising and social identity-building functions. That is why professionals should ask themselves how the community of followers of the brand benefits each follower, what is the unique value of the brand's community and why it is worthwhile for the brand's followers to keep up to date with the content.

Social networks offer strong potential to build one-to-one communications with each consumer and build online communities. The management of communities in social networks should try to achieve the following (Baird and Parasnis, 2011; WARC, 2021):

- Love and Passion. Consumers want to feel a strong emotional attachment to the brand
- Self-connection. Consumers feel a strong connection between the brand and their personal identity. The brand represents an important aspect of the consumer's self
- Interdependence. Consumers have a high level of interaction with the brand. Interactions are emotionally important to the consumer. The brands become part of important rituals in the consumer's life.
- Commitment. Consumers want to maintain a long-term relationship with the brand. If the brand is committed to customers, they will offer their loyalty.
- Intimacy. Consumers want to know a lot about the brand, the company and the people behind the brand. They appreciate a personalised and intimate knowledge of the brand.

According to the consulting firm McKinsey Report (2022, pp. 2–3), in order for brands to generate a successful community, they must activate the five elements of the 'community flywheel':

- 'First, know to what consumers your brand appeals to and what communities they are part of.
- Second, pick just a few 'hero products' that truly encapsulate the value of your brand to allow you to cut through the digital noise.
- Third, support and bring to life these hero products with exciting and authentic brand and customer stories.
- Fourth, feed the community with content to engage with and spur brand advocates to generate their own.
- Finally, make it easy to transact, both offline and online. Brands that excel at all five elements generate a fast-spinning flywheel, in which brand advocates generate conversation, engagement, and sales.'

A community-focused fashion brand is a brand that tries to identify its different customer communities and offer each one what it needs. To do this, it is important to pay attention to the segmentation and needs of each consumer group, as we saw in *Section 1* of the book. It is difficult for a large brand to serve each user individually, so you can work on micro-segmentation by looking for shared interests and similar values, which is called 'shared relevance.' Indeed, as highlighted in previous chapters, knowledge of consumer behaviour is essential to provide value and generate brand engagement.

To perform this task of brand love and brand engagement, one of the most effective elements of social communication is storytelling. The brand should focus on having a credible and consistent brand story with which the consumer can identify himself/herself.

Brands might also consider co-creating their story with their consumer in order to co-create value. Some of the actions brands can take on social media networks are:

- Post positive comments whenever a customer mentions the brand
- Encourage users to share their looks and comments
- Thank users when they share the brand's content in their community
- Ask consumers what they want, what they need and what content they would like to see.
- Start conversations to develop products or services together with the consumers

Bibliography

Baird, C.H. and Parasnis, G., 2011. From social media to social customer relationship management. *Strategy & Leadership*, *39*(5), pp. 30–37.

Cerchia, A.E., 2016. Social media – a strategy in developing customer relationship management. *Procedia Economics and Finance*, *39*, pp. 785–790.

Hootsuite, 2021. *What is social CRM?* Available at: https://blog.hootsuite.com/social-crm/#What_is_social_CRM (Accessed: 21 May 2022).

McKinsey Report, 2022. *A better way to build a brand: The community flywheel*. McKinsey. Available at: https://www.mckinsey.com/capabilities/growth-marketing-and-sales/our-insights/a-better-way-to-build-a-brand-the-community-flywheel#/.

Scheiner, M., 2024. *What is social CRM? 10 best social media CRM tools & software platforms*. Available at: https://crm.org/crmland/social-crm (Accessed: 24 October 2023).

WARC, 2021. *From discovery to purchase: The role of community commerce*. WARC. Available at: https://www.warc.com/content/article/warc-exclusive/from-discovery-to-purchase-the-role-of-community-commerce/139665 (Accessed: 23 October 2022).

8

CALENDAR, BUDGET, MONITORING AND TOOLS

Introduction

This chapter concludes the Social Media Performance Section. Once the commercial action plan, the content plan and the CRM and community plan have been developed, the focus shifts to the social media calendar. A fundamental part is budgeting. Once the budget is approved and scheduled in accordance with the general communication and marketing department, the plan can be executed. Brands can monitor the campaign(s) developed and utilise this data to measure its effectiveness and future possible improvements.

Calendar

As presented in Chapter 6, content creation plans require the development of a calendar that includes details regarding the content that is going to be published, the time and the hashtags. In addition to content calendars, companies can and should create a general social media calendar.

The general calendar of social networks unifies all the content plans of each social network, the social commercial actions (advertising campaigns) and all the campaigns the company wants to broadcast. Often, a brand may have different professionals working on creating different content plans for different campaigns. The global calendar unifies everything, and it should be in line with the brand's marketing and communication calendars.

Managing the calendar of actions and publications on social networks can be challenging for fashion brands as there are many events that should be taken into consideration.

An example of the European fashion retail events is presented in Table 8.1.

DOI: 10.4324/9781003505495-12

TABLE 8.1 Fashion retail events related to social media content

January	February	March	April
Sales campaign	Pre-launch campaign for new Spring/Summer Collection Cruise/Resort Campaign Collections	New Spring/ Summer Collection Campaign International Women's Rights Day World Recycling Day	
May	**June**	**July**	**August**
Cruise Collections Cannes Film Festival Mother's Day	Summer Sales Campaign World Oceans Day	Summer Sales Campaign	Pre-season Fall Winter and Back-to-School Campaign
September	**October**	**November**	**December**
Back-to-School Campaign Fall/Winter Season Campaign	Launching of Halloween Mini-Collections		Christmas Collection Campaign

Source: Own elaboration

In addition, beyond the aforementioned calendars, companies can have calendars that show the team's workflow with the details of the entire work process involved in developing a social media strategy. They can include information such as:

- When to start thinking about a creative and content idea for a campaign
- When will the content be produced?
- In which location should it be done?
- What kind of team should it involve?
- When should we test the videos and photos?
- When will they be published?
- When to analyse the results?

It is useful for the workflow of the calendar to present all the tasks to be performed by the social media department. For example, the company Semrush has created a 'Social Media Task Checklist' to help professionals schedule their daily, monthly and quarterly work. The activities that Semrush suggests are presented in Table 8.2.

Budget

The budget is one of the most important parts of a social media plan.

The budget varies depending on different factors such as the type of fashion brand, its size, the time frame for the social media campaign, the type and size of target that should be reached (Hootsuite, 2023; Luzon et al., 2022).

TABLE 8.2 Examples of professional tasks to be performed on social media

Daily task	*Weekly tasks*	*Monthly tasks*	*Quarterly tasks*
—Check and update your posting calendar. —Reply to comments and questions. —Monitor your brand mentions online and react to them. —Discover industry-related keywords and threads. —Check what your competitors are posting. —Monitor industry news. —Discover trending hashtags. —Monitor and comment on influencers' posts.	—Synchronise with other teams' goals and upcoming activities. —Create a posting schedule for the week. —Identify your competitors' best-performing posts. —Track the results of your ongoing ad campaigns. —Boost well-performing posts.	—Collect monthly stats. —Analyse your competitors' social strategies. —Compare your performance against your competitors. —Identify your month's successes and integrate them into your social strategy. – Define the next month's ratio of educational to entertaining content. —Research upcoming news and events that can be used to promote your product or service.	—Review and evaluate the last quarter's KPIs and see where you stand. —Make sure your brand image is consistent across all social channels. —Conduct audience analysis to see if you are targeting the right people. —Set your goals for the next quarter. —Define your KPIs for the next quarter.

Source: Semrush Blog (2018)

Companies with substantial social media marketing budgets are able to:

- Buy social media management tools
- Work with specialised agencies
- Hire professional content creators
- Carry out advertising campaigns
- Create professional content
- Hire influencers for the diffusion or creation of contents
- Have more staff for customer service across the different social networks

Based on the budget available, social media professionals will have to make decisions.

There are two questions that those who are responsible for the strategy can ask themselves: 'What is my community demanding?' and 'What impacts my community the most?'.

Table 8.3 provides an example of the elements that a social media budget should include.

TABLE 8.3 Example of the social media budget categories

Category	*Items*
Content Creation	Photos' production Video productions Shooting productions, including celebrities, models, photographers, locations Graphic design Editing Copywriting
Human Resources	Internal team Freelancers External agencies
Paid Social Media Campaigns	Ads campaigns in different social media platforms
Paid Social Media Content	Content creators Influencers Celebrities
Tools and Software	For social listening For content creation For management (monitoring and analytics) For CRM

Source: Own elaboration

Monitoring

All social media campaigns should be monitored by companies both during and after the campaigns in order to understand their effectiveness. Campaign objectives are usually presented with a set of Key Performance Indicators (KPIs) that serve for their evaluation.

KPIs are the metrics that help brands measure business objectives, performance and progress over time. Some of the most important KPIs and metrics are explained next (Hubspot, 2021):

- Engagement: This includes clicks, comments, likes and replies on your social media posts. There are also platform-specific types of engagement such as 'Saved' posts on Instagram and 'Pinned' posts on Pinterest
- Reach: The number of people who have seen any content associated with your page or profile
- Followers: This is the number of people you have on your profile who have clicked your 'Follow' button and see your content in their feeds regularly
- Impressions: This is the number of times a post from your profile or page is seen, whether or not your audience members click on it. This is often what happens when someone is scrolling through their newsfeed but not clicking on anything

- Video views: On Facebook, Snapchat, Instagram, or any other social channel with video capabilities, this is the number of views each video gets
- Profile visits: The number of people who have opened your social media page
- Mentions: This is the number of times your profile has been mentioned by audience members in their posts
- Tags: This is when your audience adds the name of your company's profile or your hashtag to another post or another profile
- Reposts: This is when a member of your audience posts a piece of your content on their profile
- Shares: These are the posts your followers and audience take from your profile and share with their network
- Clicks: This is the number of clicks on your content or account. Tracking clicks per campaign is essential to understand what drives curiosity or encourages people to buy
- Hashtag performance: What were your most-used hashtags? Which hashtags were mostly associated with your brand? Having these answers can help shape the focus of your content going forward
- Organic and paid likes: Beyond a standard 'Like' count, these interactions are attributed to paid or organic content. Given how much harder organic engagement is to gain, many brands turn to ads. Knowing these differences can help you budget both your ad spend and the time you invest in different media formats
- Sentiment: This is the measurement of how users react to your content, brand or hashtag. Did customers find your recent campaign offensive?

Motivations lead us to behave (interact) with content on social media profiles in a certain way, resulting in 'user social media behaviour.' As stated earlier, most of the actions that a user performs on social networks leave 'a trace' that can be analysed in the form of text, likes, shares, follows, views, etc. The analysis of this data is known as Big Social Data (Tuten and Solomon, 2018). All this information can be analysed from quantitative and qualitative perspectives to reach insightful knowledge that describes users' behaviour on social networks. Some of the variables that explain user behaviour (Kontu and Vecchi, 2014; Narwal, 2019; Tuten and Solomon, 2018) are:

- Time spent using social networks
- Level of interactions on each social network
- Users/brands with the most fans or followers
- Volume of views of published content
- Volume of interactions with published content
- Type of profiles sought and consumed
- Type of information sought and consumed
- Content trends

As a general guideline, for social media monitoring, it is useful to follow four key steps (Sutherland, 2020, p. 136):

- Step 1: Gather data
- Step 2: Analyse and interpret data
- Step 3: Report data
- Step 4: Use report findings to improve performance

Despite its usefulness, conducting social media research beyond the social media monitoring approach and KPIs can not only complement but also help explain the results. Section 4 of this book is dedicated to an in-depth discussion of the existing research methods that fashion brands can utilise to evaluate the performance of their social media campaigns and those of their competitors and better understand social media consumer behaviour.

Social Media Tools

There are many tools available to facilitate social media management (Geyser, 2023; Simonson, 2023). This book does not intend to make a catalogue of all of them. We will only suggest some examples relevant to the time in which this book was written.

The tools are listed by function in an alphabetical order.

Social Media Listening and Sentiment Analysis

- Brand24: A web and social media monitoring tool designed for businesses of all sizes. It provides monitoring tools for keywords, brand names and more on the web, as well as social media, forums, news websites, blogs, photos and videos
- BrandMentions: A tool to monitor brands or products on the Internet. It also enables to measure the buzz around the brand
- BrandWatch: A tool that tracks billions of conversations happening online every day, including blogs, news, forums, videos, reviews, images, etc. It allows brands and companies to understand consumer insights, trends, influencers and brand perceptions.
- BuzzSumo: A software that allows marketers to search for the most shared topics on the Internet

Social Media Content Creation

- Canva: A free graphic design platform that allows easy creation of graphical content which can be used on social media
- ContentCal: A multipurpose content marketing platform that allows to plan, create, collaborate, publish and analyse content—all from one central location

Social Media Management

- Fanpage Karma: An online tool for analysis and monitoring of social networks. It helps community managers and agencies better connect with fans and reach a growing community on social media
- Hootsuite: A web and mobile social media management platform built to engage and listen to users. It also allows analysing the results of social media performance
- Hubspot: Software to publish content, build social media campaigns, set up keywords, monitor conversations and report on the results
- Later: Social media management platform and link in bio tool for every social network. It helps to plan, analyse and publish content in advance
- Social Pilot: A social media marketing tool to increase brand awareness and traffic. It provides tailored social media automation services for marketers
- Sprout Social: A social media management and intelligence tool that helps manage conversations and identify the actionable insights that drive real business impact

Social Media CRM

- Hootsuite: It performs valuable social CRM functions. It allows the setup of a social listening programme and a consolidation of social messages from multiple platforms in a single inbox. From the inbox, it is possible to assign social messages to the appropriate team members in the relevant department.
- Hubspot: CRM tool built around the inbound marketing methodology. Hubspot aims to attract, convert and delight customers by aligning marketing, sales, customer service and operations under one platform.

Bibliography

Content Marketing Institute, 2021. *Best social media tools*. Content Marketing Institute. Available at: https://contentmarketinginstitute.com/articles/best-social-media-tools-top-marketers/ (Accessed: 12 December 2023).

Geyser, W., 2023. *Top 22 social media tools you need in your marketing arsenal*. Influencer Marketing Hub, 15 November. Available at: https://influencermarketinghub.com/social-media-tools/ (Accessed: 12 December 2023).

Hootsuite, 2023. *How to create a social media budget: Breakdown and tips*. Hootsuite, 23 July. Available at: https://blog.hootsuite.com/the-7-components-of-every-social-media-budget/ (Accessed: 12 December 2023).

Hubspot, 2021. *Choosing-KPIs*. Hubspost, 28 September. Available at: https://blog.hubspot.com/marketing/choosing-kpis (Accessed: 25 September 2022).

Kontu, H. and Vecchi, A., 2014. Why all that noise-assessing the strategic value of social media for fashion brands. *Journal of Global Fashion Marketing*, *5*(3), pp. 235–250.

Luzon, Y., Pinchover, R. and Khmelnitsky, E., 2022. Dynamic budget allocation for social media advertising campaigns: Optimization and learning. *European Journal of Operational Research*, *299*(1), pp. 223–234.

Narwal, N., 2019. Customer segmentation using social media data. *International Journal of Management, IT and Engineering*, *7*(10), pp. 117–125.

Semrush Blog, 2018. *Your ultimate social media checklist*. Semrush, 19 August. Available at: https://www.semrush.com/blog/your-ultimate-social-media-checklist-semrush/ (Accessed: 25 September 2022).

Simonson, J., 2023. 5 best social media management tools. *Forbes*, 16 November. Available at: https://www.forbes.com/advisor/business/best-social-media-management-software/ (Accessed: 12 December 2023).

Smartinsights, 2022. *Customer relationship management*. Available at: https://www.smartinsights.com/customer-relationship-management/social-crm/social-crm-strategy/ (Accessed: 9 December 2023).

Sutherland, K.E., 2020. *Strategic social media management: Theory and practice*. Springer Nature.

Tuten, T.L. and Solomon, M.R., 2018. *Social media marketing* (pp. 1–448). Sage Publications.

SECTION 4

Social Media Research Opportunities and Methodologies

The aim of this section is to provide a general overview on the opportunities and challenges of conducting social media research and to present four methodologies that can be useful for fashion firms' social media analysis.

Social media research can be highly valuable for companies in order to gain insights (Rogers, 2021) as it represents a goldmine of data, which is:

- High in volume
- (Sometimes) freely available
- Multimodal (presents itself in different formats)
- Constantly updated

The analysis of the *high volume of data* available on social media channels can provide firms with insightful knowledge regarding consumers' demographics, their opinions, preferences, needs, beliefs and habits. Such data can be precious in guiding and improving decision-making, enhancing business processes and detecting trends. The insights extracted represent an opportunity to create value by getting to know the consumers, who play an active role in deciding the success or failure of products and services.

Data on social media can be *freely available*, reducing the need to prompt users to gain insights from them. This represents an opportunity to collect a large volume of data at a low cost. However, it should be noted that sometimes data can only be accessed through a fee or if you are the account owner.

The array of *formats* in which social media users can communicate and freely express themselves on social media offers a variety of data for analysis, such as textual, visual and video content; users' profile pages and activities such as likes and

DOI: 10.4324/9781003505495-13

shares (Mayr and Weller, 2017). The analysis that involves different data formats is called multimodal analysis.

A further benefit of conducting research on social media is *timeliness* and the availability of *updated information*. Firms can monitor users' information in real time, allowing them to make timely decisions and make predictions based on users' behaviour (Schreck and Keim, 2013).

Thus, information extracted from social media channels can be beneficial for businesses to gain actionable knowledge and a competitive edge and for the research community for doing longitudinal studies.

Despite the advantages, social media implies some challenges.

Collecting and analysing *high volumes* of data can be complex, time-consuming and costly. Another major challenge of social media research is *interpretation*. Social media is highly context-dependent. Hence, it is important to not de-contextualize the data collected. Interpreting the way in which users express themselves on social media is not always straightforward. For example regarding a post that states, *'I love this bag, it looks great, but I would never buy it for myself'*— although it includes positive words, such as 'love' and 'great,' it expresses the unwillingness to purchase the product. Hence, the data available must be analysed with caution and attention.

Moreover, the wide use of jargon, abbreviations, emojis and memes can make the interpretation difficult as they are utilised differently by users (Highfield and Leaver, 2016; Schreck and Keim, 2013).

Lastly, it should be considered that social media content does not always represent real life, real opinions and intention; thus, caution should be taken when drawing insights.

The easy access to data should not come at the cost of the policies of each social media channel and important ethical questions. Although ethical concerns are not the focus of this manual, they should not be dismissed when embarking on social media analysis. Crucial aspects should be considered in order to conduct ethical research, such as the nature of data collected from social media platforms, whether it is public or private and compliance with local laws, such as GDPR in Europe. Furthermore, it might be necessary to receive informed consent and to anonymize the posts (Kozinets and Gretzel, 2021).

Thus, although it can be useful, measuring social media performance and gaining actionable insights from the data collected can be challenging and should be approached systematically in accordance to the questions of interest and the amount of data necessary, taking into consideration possible biases and ethical issues.

The section 'Social Media Research Opportunities and Methodologies' is conceptualised as a starting point for students, researchers and practitioners interested in learning about social media research analysis in fashion. It is thought of as a reference manual, which summarises relevant academic work on social media research for those who are relatively new to the topic and who wish to discover and navigate various methodologies.

As discussed in the previous chapters of this manual, social media platforms evolve, thus this section does not focus on how to apply the methodologies on specific platforms. Although acknowledging that each platform has its unique features and affordances, it discusses the overreaching general opportunities, challenges and principles to conduct social media research by presenting different methods that can be applied.

Furthermore, this section fits within the overall manual's aim of exploring the synergy between fashion academia and industry by bringing them closer through a topic of mutual interest.

Conducting social media research beyond the social media benchmark approach and KPIs can not only complement but also help explain and enrich the results. Therefore, this manual presents in detail four methodologies that can be useful for fashion firms' social media analysis. Each of the subsequent chapters is dedicated to one methodology, which, from the authors' experience, can be useful for fashion social media analysis:

- Chapter 9: Netnography
- Chapter 10: Visual analysis
- Chapter 11: Sentiment analysis
- Chapter 12: Argumentation analysis

After reading this section, you will:

- Be exposed to four possible research methods useful for in-depth fashion social media analysis
- Understand how to select the needed method according to your research goals
- Explore an example from the academic literature that shows how the method has been applied
- Be able to apply the methodology of interest while following the guidelines, which are derived from a summary of the work of various academics

Bibliography

Highfield, T. and Leaver, T., 2016. Instagrammatics and digital methods: Studying visual social media, from selfies and GIFs to memes and emoji. *Communication Research and Practice*, *2*(1), pp. 47–62.

Kozinets, R.V. and Gretzel, U., 2021. Commentary: Artificial intelligence: The marketer's dilemma. *Journal of Marketing*, *85*(1), pp. 156–159.

Mayr, P. and Weller, K., 2017. Think before you collect: Setting up a data collection approach for social media studies. In *The Sage handbook of social media research methods* (pp. 107–124). Sage.

Rogers, R. A. 2021. Visual media analysis for Instagram and other online platforms. *Big Data & Society*. https://doi.org/10.1177/20539517211022370

Schreck, T. and Keim, D., 2013. Visual analysis of social media data. *Computer*, *46*(5), pp. 68–75. http://dx.doi.org/10.1109/MC.2012.430

Symon, G., Pritchard, K. and Hine, C., eds., 2021. *Research methods for digital work and organisation: Investigating distributed, multi-modal, and mobile work*. Oxford University Press.

9

NETNOGRAPHY

Introduction

Understanding social media requires a holistic and deep cultural insight. As we will see throughout this chapter, netnography research enables us to address such a need.

The term netnography derives from the combination of the words 'net' referring to the Internet and 'ethnography,' which refers to the study of culture and society (Kozinets, 2012). This methodology was developed in 1995 by professor Kozinets as a response to the change in social interactions and to the increased use of the Internet.

Because social network analysis focuses on relational data—the relationship between actors in a network—there is an obvious connection with netnography (Kozinets, 2012). The growth of virtual communities, social media and consumer activity on such channels highly contributed to the development of netnography, attracting the interest of both academics and practitioners (Bartl et al., 2016).

Netnography is a qualitative research methodology that 'adapts ethnographic research techniques to study the cultures and communities that are emerging through computer-mediated communication' (Kozinets, 2002, p. 62). It is a participant-observational method that requires the researcher's immersion in the community under study through an iterative process (Kozinets, 2002). It represents a spontaneous way to unlock cultural codes, reach a deep cultural understanding and recognise data as cultural data (Kozinets and Gretzel, 2022).

The aim is to deeply understand the rich communicative and symbolic world of social media and dive deep into its contextual meaning beyond KPIs and quantitative (statistical) analysis. This method involves monitoring information that occurs naturally on social platforms to gain in-depth knowledge of a group of individuals.

DOI: 10.4324/9781003505495-14

The data in netnography derives from the information shared online through multiple devices (Kozinets, 2016).

Because netnography takes place in the context in which the communication originally took place, it is an unobtrusive way to understand the consumer behaviour. The unobtrusive nature of methods, gain insights also from communities and individuals that are less likely to share their opinions and investigate sensitive topics that can be hard to address.

Furthermore, netnography can be combined with other research methods, such as interviews and surveys, as it benefits from the multimodal nature of social media. It can be used as a relatively fast and convenient data collection method (Bartl et al., 2016; Kozinets, 2002; Wu, 2021). Various tools such as Google Groups, Google Trends, Google Social Search, X (formerly known as Twitter) Search, NVivo, Flickr and DeviantArt can also be utilised to assist netnography research in sourcing, tracking, collecting, reducing and visualising data. To refer to the use of tools in netnography research, Kozinets (2010) coined the term 'computationally assisted netnography.'

Although netnography research has many advantages, it is important to consider the following elements.

First, despite the possibility of downloading data directly from the platforms, netnography should not be limited to the act of downloading communications; instead, the researcher should observe how the conversation evolves within the context. The researcher's engagement role can take place at different levels: it can range from a passive approach, where the researcher passively observes the community, to an active approach, where the researcher actively contributes to the discussion by interacting with the members (Wu, 2021).

Second, the researcher should not collect all the data available on a topic of interest. Indeed, social media offers an overload of data; yet, data should be collected selectively.

Third, conducting netnography implies important ethical considerations that cannot be dismissed. Ethics in netnography can be complicated as the lines between public and private spheres are blurred on the Internet. Moreover, the content collected represents a copy of individuals' identities. Hence, it is important to conduct transparent research; for example the researcher can disclose his/her presence, ensure confidentiality and anonymity and ask permission to quote the collected material (Kozinets and Gretzel, 2022).

Netnography in Fashion

As a market and consumer research method, netnography can be an extremely relevant method for the fashion industry to conduct social media research. Studies have shown that it can provide managers with insightful findings for marketing, communication and general managerial purposes (Bartl et al., 2016; Kozinets, 2010).

Consumers' behaviour, activities, habits, preferences and needs are reflected in social media. Hence, netnography can help bring to light customers' consumption habits, their feedback, shopping motivations, information regarding their decision-making process, cultural values and symbols. It is also a valuable method to identify consumers' identities, such as social media persona, and different types of users. For example, a fashion firm might want to pinpoint the lead user of a product. This can be a challenging yet crucial task as the lead users are at the forefront of the market trends (Belz and Baumbach, 2010). The data collected through netnography, such as product usage and customer feedback, enables to also identify trends and directions for product development. It supports the identification of the firm's strengths, weaknesses and positioning strategy and helps conduct competitive analysis.

Heinonen and Medberg (2018) provide a list of key questions (Table 9.1) as a guideline to start delving into netnography research.

The next section provides details on how to conduct the netnography research.

TABLE 9.1 Considerations for managerial use of netnography

Key questions	*Considerations*
What research should be done?	What is the research objective? What information is needed? What other methods could be used instead?
How should the research be done?	Should netnography be combined with other methods? Is passive observation sufficient, or is active participation preferable? How will the data be collected and analysed? Is textual information sufficient, or should other types of data be retrieved?
Where should the research be done?	Which are the most suitable online domains for data collection? What are the pros and cons of different online domains? Should there be triangulation across different domains or an in-depth study of one domain?
Who should do the research, and who should be researched?	Who should be responsible for data collection and analysis? Do existing staff have sufficient knowledge about netnography? Should existing or potential customers be studied? Should actors other than customers be studied?
When should the research be done?	When in time should the study be conducted? What should be the length of the study? Should it be a one-time collection or a long-term longitudinal research process?

Source: Heinonen and Medberg (2018)

Netnography Analysis

Conducting netnography requires (i) engagement of the researcher(s) who immerse themselves in the research, (ii) attention to developments as it evolves with the digital advances and (iii) attention to ethical principles (Kozinets and Gretzel, 2023).

Netnography is performed through four basic steps, which occur in overlap with one another in an iterative process:

(1) Research inquiry
(2) Data collection
(3) Data analysis and interpretation
(4) Research communication

These steps are further detailed in six interconnected stages called movements, as detailed next, which enable to provide an initial structure to the research.

Step 1: Research Inquiry

This first step starts with the movement of:

(a) Initiation: Identify significant and innovative research question(s) or problem(s)

Step 2: Data Collection

The second step involves three movements: (b) Immersion, (c) investigation and (d) interaction.

(b) Immersion: Search insightful data and indexing. Data is examined, and notes are taken
(c) Investigation: Identify social media sources relevant to the research and decide on which sites to focus on. A possible way to approach this is through a netnography landscape defined as 'a visual representation of sites containing communications relevant to a particular research question' (Kozinets, 2019, p. 140)
(d) Interaction: Explicit questioning and engagement with online participants to clarify topics, for example, through interviews

Step 3: Data Analysis

Analysing the data implies breaking down the dataset into elements, assigning codes and finding patterns.

(e) Integration: The data is combined and interpreted in order to answer the research question or problem identified in Step 1

Step 4: Research Communication

The final step involves

(f) Incarnation: Communicate the findings in a relevant way

Example of Netnographic Analysis from a Fashion Study

This study provides an example of an academic study that has adopted netnography research in order to give an overview of the steps followed to collect and analyse the data.

The study carried out by Parrot et al. (2015) titled 'Online behaviour of luxury fashion brand advocates' provides an analysis of the influence online fashion communities have on purchase intention and brand love by adopting a netnography approach.

Research inquiry: Identify the behaviours and characteristics of online brand advocates by observing community members' interactions, conversations and activities.

1. Selection of Communities to Study

Four sites (The Purse Forum, The Fashion Spot, The Bag Forum and The Shoe Forum) were selected according to the following criteria suggested by Kozinets (2002):

- Relevant information about fashion and fashion accessories
- Highly active community members
- Interactivity between participants
- Richness of the information posted by members

2. A Researcher Subscribed and Became a Member of the Four Selected Sites

- Observation phase: Adopt a non-participative role to study behaviours and characteristics of online brand advocates. Observations were conducted between April 2010 and February 2011.
- Participant observation: The researcher openly and actively participated in conversations as a community member from April to June 2011.

3. Data Collection and Analysis

- Observation of unique posts by active members: 75 successful visits were made, lasting an average of two hours
- The empirical data was collected in the form of texts and images

- A log was created for each visit, recording the date, time and duration of the forum visit in addition to a narrative reflection of the content of the posts and identification of key themes
- Data selection: Focused on relevant threads relating to four aspects of brand advocacy that are involvement, brand love, brand commitment and brand loyalty. A total of 234 meaningful blog posts were identified for further analysis
- These posts were then analysed using visual and interpretive content analysis

4. Ethical Considerations of the Authors

The researcher did not announce himself in phase one of the data collection; yet, it was reported that findings were harvested from open forums/conversations, where members are aware that their written messages/opinions are available on public space (Xun and Reynolds, 2010).

Bibliography

Bartl, M., Kannan, V.K. and Stockinger, H., 2016. A review and analysis of literature on netnography research. *International Journal of Technology Marketing, 11*(2), pp. 165–196.

Belz, F.M. and Baumbach, W., 2010. Netnography as a method of lead user identification. *Creativity and Innovation Management, 19*(3), pp. 304–313.

Heinonen, K. and Medberg, G., 2018. Netnography as a tool for understanding customers: Implications for service research and practice. *Journal of Services Marketing, 32*(6), pp. 657–679.

Kozinets, R.V., 2002. The field behind the screen: Using netnography for marketing research in online communities. *Journal of Marketing Research, 39*(1), pp. 61–72.

Kozinets, R.V., 2010. Netnography: The marketer's secret weapon. *White Paper*, pp. 1–13.

Kozinets, R.V., 2012. Marketing netnography: Prom/ot (ulgat) ing a new research method. *Methodological Innovations Online, 7*(1), pp. 37–45.

Kozinets, R.V., 2015. *Netnography: Redefined* (pp. 1–297). Sage.

Kozinets, R.V. 2016. *Netnography*. The Blackwell Encyclopedia of Sociology. Edited by George Ritzer, John Wiley & Sons, Ltd. DOI: 10.1002/9781405165518.wbeos0782

Kozinets, R.V., 2019. Netnography: The essential guide to qualitative social media research. *Netnography*, pp. 1–472.

Kozinets, R.V. and Gretzel, U. 2022. Netnography. *In book: Encyclopedia of Tourism Management and Marketing*. http://dx.doi.org/10.4337/9781800377486.netnography

Kozinets, R.V. and Gretzel, U., 2023. Netnography evolved: New contexts, scope, procedures and sensibilities. *Annals of Tourism Research, 104*.

Parrott, G., Danbury, A. and Kanthavanich, P., 2015. Online behaviour of luxury fashion brand advocates. *Journal of Fashion Marketing and Management, 19*(4), pp. 360–383.

Wu, D., 2021. More than a solo method: Netnography's capacity to enhance offline research methods. *Area, 54*(1), pp. 88–95.

Xun, J. and Reynolds, J., 2010. Applying netnography to market research: The case of the online forum. *Journal of Targeting, Measurement and Analysis for Marketing, 18*, pp. 17–31.

10
VISUAL ANALYSIS

Introduction

The Web is becoming increasingly visual. Images are being widely adopted as they are a quick, expressive and timely form of communication. Visuals have always been part of individuals' life; the emergence of new technologies and technological affordances have made visuals widely accessible and shareable.

Smartphones with integrated cameras enable individuals to take photos of their daily lives and easily share them on platforms such as social media channels, offering a vast database of images. Furthermore, visuals are socially embedded, and they can provide many insights regarding people's lives, their social persona and relationships.

When sharing images, individuals consider different aspects, including their expected audience, affordances and aesthetical requirements of the platform on which they are sharing and the communication habits of others, offering a wide range of information of the phenomenon under study. Thus, visual research has attracted growing interest by communication scholars (Banks, 2001; Highfield and Leaver, 2016; Lobinger et al., 2020).

Data in the form of visuals offers both opportunities and challenges for research.

In terms of opportunities, visuals (Milanesi et al., 2022; Russmann and Svensson, 2017):

- Are a dynamic form of content
- Are a direct and often immediate form of communication that can be processed extremely fast by individuals
- Can suggest reality, generate casual relationships and strengthen interactions
- Are relatively easy to understand and interpret

DOI: 10.4324/9781003505495-15

- Have a high potential to attract individuals' attention and transfer information rapidly
- Afford highly informative, strategic and reflective communication

Visuals also imply some challenges (Niedere and Colombo, 2019), such as:

- The circulation of images, moving and copying them across platforms and the possibility to modify and comment on them, although being opportunities, make them transient and ephemeral
- Sometimes, the meanings linked to visuals remain hidden and hard to interpret
- In different cultural contexts, the visuals can be interpreted differently

Such challenges, if properly addressed, represent an opportunity for visual research to gain in-depth findings (Highfield and Leaver, 2016; Lai and Perminiene, 2020). Text and images should not be considered as competing forms of communication and should not be considered in isolation. Indeed, textual and visual information should be treated as complementing forms of communication in order to reach a comprehensive understanding of the phenomenon under study (Brantner et al., 2013).

Visual Research on Social Media

The diverse type of content that can be shared on social media has required 'researchers to broaden and diversify the way in which social media is examined and addressed' (Highfield and Leaver, 2016, p. 49).

Sharing images and videos on social media has become a mainstream practice, and for various channels, such as Instagram and TikTok, it is the platform's focus, representing an extremely interesting avenue for communication research (Belk and Kozinets, 2005).

The visuals available for research take various forms. Broadly, we can distinguish between content that firms share and the content users share, the so-called user-generated content (UGC). For firms, social media provides the possibility to deliver highly impactful communication through images and attract individuals' attention (Milanesi et al., 2022). For individuals, it is an opportunity to express themselves and relate to other users, as the act of sharing visuals impacts not only the way in which we perceive ourselves but also the way in which we relate to others and our relationships with brands. In several cases, these two forms are interconnected, for example, when brands adopt UGC in their official social media channels (Naeem and Ozuem, 2022).

Visual analysis on social media channels is suggested to overcome some of the challenges typical of visual research. If collecting visuals was a costly and time-consuming procedure (Banks, 2001), the proliferation of visuals on social media has helped overcome these issues. Furthermore, visuals on social media can be accompanied by other forms of communication, including written text, hashtags and emoticons. The multimodal nature of social media posts enables to frame, filter and edit images before they are shared. As mentioned earlier, sometimes, it can be challenging to depict the meaning of visuals. Other sources that accompany visuals on social media, such as the post's caption, the hashtags and the tags, can support the interpretation (Karamalak et al., 2021; Klostermann et al., 2018). For example social tagging, the practice of associating information through tags, can provide rich information to marketers regarding users' feelings and brand associations in support of visual interpretation (Nam and Kannan, 2014).

Visual Analysis in Fashion

Fashion communication and visual communication are highly interconnected. Fashion brands are increasingly relying on visual content in order to attract consumers' attention as it is an engaging form of communication. Moreover, it responds to consumers' desire for visual content (Milanesi et al., 2022). This has led to social media being saturated with visual content; hence, it is of extreme importance for fashion brands to adopt an effective visual strategy in order to attract and maintain users' attention (Kusumasondjaja, 2020).

Visual content analysis is suggested to provide managerial implications for fashion brands and offer guidance on how to develop compelling visual content, including (a) design principles to attract individuals' attention, (b) map an issue of interest and (c) understand consumers' attitudes towards their visual strategy and trend forecasting (Kusumasondjaja, 2020). These points are hereafter discussed.

a. Design Principles

Visual analysis can help a fashion brand identify visual design principles that are effective to attract consumers' attention and portray its values (Lee et al., 2018; Milanesi et al., 2022). As a form of 'owned media,' brands can disseminate their own content and communicate their values on social media. Visual research studies have offered firms interesting insights on how to manage their visual presence on social media, the type of visual stimuli that are effective in communicating their values and directions on how to make the most of the persuasive power of the visual images through different design principles (Kusumasondjaja, 2020; Lee et al., 2018). For example visual analysis can help answer questions such as: How should a sustainable brand's social media page look like in order to portray the value of sustainability? How can visuals elicit consumers' responses from social media? What kind of visuals receive more engagement or lead to purchase?

Research studies employing visual analysis have provided some insightful findings to these questions, for example regarding visual aesthetics (Kusumasondjaja, 2020) and visual complexity (Lee et al., 2018).

Visual aesthetics refers to 'the pictorial attractiveness that conveys a clear and unique image or pleasing appearance of an image or object' (Kusumasondjaja, 2020, p. 17). Generally, visual aesthetics can be classified in:

(1) Classical aesthetics, which refers to regular, clear and symmetric designs
(2) Expressive aesthetics, which refers to the creativity of a design

Presentation modality refers to the form in which the message is delivered, such as in the form of text, video or a combination of them:

(1) A lean modality refers to static content in the form of an image
(2) A rich modality refers to dynamic video content.

Kusumasondjaja (2020) shows that expressive aesthetics can be more relevant than classic aesthetics for luxury brands on Instagram as individuals experience mood enhancement. Moreover, video content is found to perform better in terms of likes and comments compared to static visual content.

The study of visual complexity refers to 'the perceptual degree of complexity of the visual characteristics, including the number of elements, patterns, and symmetrical organisation of the image' (Lee et al., 2018, p. 451). Choosing the appropriate level of visual complexity is shown to trigger positive reactions (Lee et al., 2018). For example, on social media, images with plain backgrounds and with limited products are suggested to be effective for well-known luxury brands as they emphasise the product providing it a sense of luxury. Whereas unfamiliar brands should start with complex images as the larger number of resources provides viewers the chance to develop new associations (Lee et al., 2018).

b. Map an Issue of Interest

An appropriate visual analysis enables to map an issue of interest. Niederer (2018) in his research introduces an approach for issue mapping for fashion using digital methods. It involves different techniques for online image research to map various positions of a story and map different sides of how fashion is represented:

(1) How sustainable fashion is represented
(2) Compare and map different queries such as 'sustainable fashion' and 'ethical fashion'
(3) Identify how an issue is represented throughout time

c. Consumers' Attitudes and Trend Forecasting

Visual communication in fashion is especially important as it portrays social movements, trends, fads, consumer habits and needs (Lai and Perminiene, 2020). It can help answer questions regarding consumers' feelings and product associations, for example by detecting how and when the brand's logo is utilised.

Visual Content Analysis

Visuals cannot be 'read' as written text, as they do not follow grammatical rules. With time, we learn to associate visuals with meanings in order to 'read them.' However, visuals are context-dependent and often require a high degree of interpretation (Banks, 2001). Thus, visuals require a systematic analysis in order to gain insightful findings by reducing bias.

In order to provide a guideline on how to conduct visual analyses, the approaches suggested by Lobinger (2017) are presented, who distinguishes between

(i) Approaches that imply the examination *of* visual media content
(ii) Approaches that adopt visuals *for* research purposes

(i) Approaches Which Imply the Examination of Visual Media Content

Visual content collected on social media lends itself to both qualitative and quantitative analyses.

To avoid trivialising the meaning of images and address their polysemic nature, there are two approaches to developing categories for visual content analysis (Lobinger, 2017):

1. Create the categories from visual theoretical concepts
2. Support the quantitative analysis with the qualitative analysis in order to reach an understanding of the evident and latent meanings of the images.

a. Qualitative Approaches

Qualitative approaches:

> Pay close attention to the idiosyncrasies of the single picture, focusing on its aesthetic features and compositional representation techniques, on the history and visual symbolism of the depicted motifs, and on how the single motifs within a picture work together to create meaning.
>
> *(Lobinger, 2017, p. 1)*

The most popular qualitative research methods in visual communication are iconography/iconology and visual semiotics.

Iconography and Iconology

Iconography is an approach that enables the analysis of the content and meanings of visuals (Müller, 2012). In iconography, the visual is examined in its original context as a historical source in order to discern the culture and society of the period in which the visual was created. This method, originally developed by art and cultural historians, involves three main steps (Lobinger, 2017):

- The first step involves describing the image without cultural references
- The second step implies an iconological interpretation that requires the consultation of other sources
- The final step involves an immersion in the visual material supported by an extensive knowledge of the symbols

Visual Semiotics

Semiotics is the study of signs. Visual semiotics focuses on understanding how 'pictures create meaning' (Lobinger, 2017, p. 3). It goes beyond the analysis of the images, and it considers their context in order to reach a critical insight of their meaning. Widely adopted to examine advertisements, it considers the role of image–text relations and the dominant visual codes for interpretation (Hand, 2016).

b. Quantitative Approaches

Quantitative Visual Content Analysis

Visual content analysis 'counts and analyses how frequently certain visual codes occur in a defined set of sample images' (Milanesi et al., 2022, p. 4). Quantitative visual content analysis is useful for comparative research as it enables to systematically identify patterns in visuals. It follows the traditional steps of quantitative analysis of written text:

- Sampling
- Developing coding categories
- Assigning codes
- Measuring validity and reliability
- Data analysis and interpretation

(ii) Approaches That Adopt Visuals for Research Purposes

Although the focus of this chapter is on visual analysis of images, it is important to mention that visual methods also involve approaches that utilise visuals for research purposes, the so-called 'creative methods,' which utilise visuals as stimuli and rely on their potential to elicit information from individuals. Examples are visual/photo elicitation and visual card sorting (Lobinger, 2017).

Visual Elicitation

Visual elicitation involves the adoption of visual material—for example photos and videos as stimuli to elicit a response from an interview participant. This method is valuable as it enables research topics that could be quite complicated to be researched, and it helps to dive deep into individuals' interpretations. The material can be either created or selected by the researcher or by the participants (Lobinger, 2017).

Visual Card Sorting

Card sorting procedures are utilised to understand how individuals organise knowledge by studying the way in which they sort items in relation to each other. In open card sorting, participants freely create and name categories, whereas in closed card sorting, they follow predefined groups. The results can be analysed both qualitatively or quantitatively, and they are often integrated with interviews, for example, through visual elicitation (Lobinger, 2017).

Multimodal and Cross-Sectional Research on Social Media

Visual content on social media rarely occurs in isolation. Usually, it is multimodal, meaning it is embedded with other forms of content such as text and emojis. Thus, visual analysis often entails acknowledging the relations of images with other forms of communication (Lobinger, 2017; Pearce et al., 2020). Images are networked, meaning they are not standalone objects, rather, they are networked by individuals who like, comment and tag the image, different platforms, search engines, hashtags and timestamp. Hence, images should be analysed as part of their network as they provide a broader view to the analysis (Niedere and Colombo, 2019). For example quantitative metrics such as likes and shares can provide engagement insights, whereas 'networkedness' of images linked by hashtags and/or reactions can help answer questions regarding which sentiments cluster with which images (Pearce et al., 2020; Rogers, 2021).

Moreover, establishing the meaning of an image often requires considering the platform on which it is posted as each platform can present the same topic differently (Niederer, 2018). By acknowledging the affordance of platforms, cross-platform analysis, which is the study of 'still and moving images across two or more social media platforms' (Pearce et al., 2020, p. 161), enables to understand how a phenomenon is depicted on different channels and collect rich information.

When conducting the research across multiple platforms, it can be challenging to not lose focus. For example although hashtags are utilised on Instagram and X (formerly known as Twitter), caution should be taken in analysing them in the same way, as on Instagram they are usually utilised more freely than on Twitter. Hence, when conducting research across multiple platforms, it is important to consider that different objects might have different affordances depending on the channel in which they are used (Pearce et al., 2020). Furthermore, the way in which the visuals appear on the social media feed also depends on algorithm processes, which often remain obscure to the researcher (Hand, 2017).

Two possible approaches for analysis are the dominant and the chronological approach (Rogers, 2021):

1. The dominant image approach focuses on the image that is initially dominant from the array in terms of format and message. Otherwise, it can also focus on the opposite of the dominant (e.g. competing hashtags)
2. The chronological approach analyses the images by date, labelling the clusters at the transition points and periods. This kind of visual analysis can point to style trends (Rogers, 2021)

Example of Visual Analysis from a Fashion Study

An example of an academic study that has adopted visual analysis is hereafter presented in order to give an overview of the steps followed to collect and analyse data.

The study 'How do you depict sustainability? An analysis of images posted on Instagram by sustainable fashion companies' from Milanesi et al. (2022) investigates how sustainability is represented on Instagram by sustainable fashion companies.

Study Aims:

1. Identify how sustainability is depicted on Instagram by fashion companies
2. Identify the effects of brands' visuals in terms of digital engagement

Approach adopted: Visual content analysis

Step 1: Select the brands of interest: Stella McCartney and Patagonia
Step 2: Identify the platform(s) for analysis: Instagram
Step 3: Decide which content to extract for analysis (only visuals or multimodal content): Multimodal
Step 4: Data collection timeframe: Pictures published from July 1 to December 31, 2019 were collected from both brands' Instagram accounts
Step 5: Sample considerations:

- What is a manageable sample size to answer the research question(s)?: In total, 345 images were downloaded
- Conduct manual search or with tools to identify the relevant posts: The software 4K Stogram was utilised

Step 6: Data collection: Registered on Excel, the URL of the pictures, date of picture, the caption, the hashtag, number of likes and comments, image category

Step 7: Analysis (i) Content analysis was used to develop a coding guidebook. As a result of the classification of the visual content, ten content categories were identified: Nature & landscape, outdoor & adventure, architecture & building, animals, people & animals, fashion photo shoot, fashion items, fashion events, other.

Step 8: Analysis (ii) Quantitative analysis with SPSS to detect differences between the brands.

Main results:

In terms of engagement, the images that portray the environmental dimension of sustainability collect the highest number of likes.

The two brands adopt different visual strategies to depict sustainability:

- Patagonia utilises nature-centric images
- Stella McCartney shows a strong connection to fashion activities, such as photo shoots, fashion shows and events
- Both brands do not portray the production methods through the images

Bibliography

Banks, M., 2001. *Visual methods in social research* (pp. 1–201). Sage Publications.

Belk, R.W. and Kozinets, R.V., 2005. Videography in marketing and consumer research. *Qualitative Market Research: An International Journal*, *8*(2), pp. 128–141.

Brantner C., Geise S. and Lobinger K. 2013. Fractured Paradigm? Theories, Concepts and Methodology of Visual Framing Research: A Systematic Review. *Paper presented at the Annual Conference of the International Communication Association (ICA) "Challenging Communication Research"*. London. June 17–21.

Hand, M., 2016. Visuality in social media: Researching images, circulations and practices. In *The Sage handbook of social media research methods* (Vol. 1, pp. 215–231). Sage.

Highfield, T. and Leaver, T., 2016. Instagrammatics and digital methods: Studying visual social media, from selfies and GIFs to memes and emoji. *Communication Research and Practice*, *2*(1), pp. 47–62.

Karamalak, O., Kalbaska, N. and Cantoni, L., 2021. What do hashtags afford in digital fashion communication? An exploratory study on Gucci-related hashtags on Twitter and Instagram. *Semiotica*, *2021*(243), pp. 325–351.

Klostermann, J., Plumeyer, A., Böger, D. and Decker, R., 2018. Extracting brand information from social networks: Integrating image, text, and social tagging data. *International Journal of Research in Marketing*, *35*(4), pp. 538–556.

Kusumasondjaja, S., 2020. Exploring the role of visual aesthetics and presentation modality in luxury fashion brand communication on Instagram. *Journal of Fashion Marketing and Management: An International Journal*, *24*(1), pp. 15–31.

Lai, Y. and Perminiene, M., 2020. Embracing imperfection: Contemporary fashion communication and consumer well-being. *Journal of Fashion Marketing and Management: An International Journal*, *24*(4), pp. 685–703.

Lee, J.E., Hur, S. and Watkins, B., 2018. Visual communication of luxury fashion brands on social media: Effects of visual complexity and brand familiarity. *Journal of Brand Management*, *25*, pp. 449–462.

Lobinger, K., 2017. Visual research methods. In *The international encyclopedia of communication research methods* (pp. 1–10). Sage.

Lobinger K., Venema R. and Kaufhold A. 2020. Hybrid Repertoires of Photo Sharing: Exploring the Complexities of Young Adults' Photo-Sharing Practices. *Visual Communication*. 1–24. https://doi.org/https://doi.org/10.1177/1470357219894038

Milanesi, M., Kyrdoda, Y. and Runfola, A., 2022. How do you depict sustainability? An analysis of images posted on Instagram by sustainable fashion companies. *Journal of Global Fashion Marketing*, *13*(2), pp. 101–115.

Müller, M.G., 2012. Iconography and iconology as a visual method and approach. In *The Sage handbook of visual research methods* (pp. 283–297). London: Sage.

Naeem, M. and Ozuem, W., 2022. Understanding the different types of UGC participants and social context for fashion brands: Insights from social media platforms. *Qualitative Market Research: An International Journal*, *25*(2), pp. 181–204.

Nam, H. and Kannan, P.K., 2014. The informational value of social tagging networks. *Journal of Marketing*, *78*(4), pp. 21–40.

Niederer, S., 2018. *Networked images: Visual methodologies for the digital age*. Amsterdam University of Applied Sciences.

Niederer, S. and Colombo, G., 2019. Visual methodologies for networked images: Designing visualizations for collaborative research, cross-platform analysis, and public participation. *Diseña*, *14*, pp. 40–67.

Pearce, W., Özkula, S.M., Greene, A.K., Teeling, L., Bansard, J.S., Omena, J.J. and Rabello, E.T., 2020. Visual cross-platform analysis: Digital methods to research social media images. *Information, Communication & Society*, *23*(2), pp. 161–180.

Rogers, R., 2021. Visual media analysis for Instagram and other online platforms. *Big Data & Society*, *8*(1), https://doi.org/10.1177/20539517211022370.

Russmann, U. and Svensson, J., 2017. Introduction to visual communication in the age of social media: Conceptual, theoretical and methodological challenges. *Media and Communication*, *5*(4), pp. 1–5.

11

SENTIMENT ANALYSIS

Introduction

Information can be broadly distinguished into facts and opinions. Facts are objective expressions, whereas opinions are subjective expressions. Opinions can be of very different types. In sentiment analysis research, also called opinion mining, the focus is usually on opinions that express either positive or negative sentiments (Liu, 2010).

Before the advent of the World Wide Web, individuals would ask families and friends for their opinions before making a decision, and organisations would conduct surveys and focus groups for decision-making and strategic purposes.

The World Wide Web has revolutionised the traditional dynamics of opinion sharing as individuals have the possibility to share their opinions, experiences and reviews of products and services online. Such information in the form of user-generated content is available to other individuals for review and as a source for decision-making. Firms have access to vast amounts of individuals' opinions regarding their products, services and as well as those of their competitors. If you ever left a comment with your feedback on a brand's product or service, it is likely that the content has been used by the brand for sentiment analysis.

The easy access to individuals' opinions has raised the interest of academia and organisations in sentiment analysis as they are increasingly getting interested in predicting consumers' attitudes and gaining actionable insights (Cambria et al., 2017; Liu, 2010).

Sentiment analysis refers to the detection of an individual's attitude towards a tangible or intangible object (Cambria et al., 2017; Mohammad, 2017). It is defined as 'the study of opinions, sentiments, and emotions expressed in text' (Liu, 2010, p. 3). An opinion is a positive or negative view, attitude or emotion. An individual

DOI: 10.4324/9781003505495-16

can hold an opinion about anything, including products, services, topics, events, individuals and organisations. Generally, these are referred to as objects, and the individual who holds the opinion is called opinion holder. The orientation of an opinion, also referred to as sentiment orientation, polarity of opinion or semantic orientation, determines whether the opinion is positive, neutral or negative (Liu, 2010).

Sentiment analysis enables to also assess the strength of the opinion. Moreover, it allows to detect a range of consumer emotions such as sadness and joy (Cambria et al., 2017; Mohammad, 2017).

Sentiment analysis can be conducted manually or automatically with the support of machines. Both ways entail advantages and challenges (Wankhade et al., 2022).

Manual analysis reduces the possible error terms of interpretation. For example it is easier for a person to detect irony or sarcasm, whereas for machine analysis, it can be challenging to detect language nuances and possibly lead to biased findings as the comments that cannot be classified as positive or negative are classified as neutral (Pantano et al., 2019). For example an individual expressing a negative feedback on a dress by ironically saying 'This dress fits just perfectly' could be erroneously interpreted as a positive comment by a machine, whereas an individual would be able to depict the ironic tone of the comment from the context and therefore identify it as a negative comment. This is because figurative expressions such as irony and sarcasm can be challenging to analyse as it is not always possible to determine valence from words in isolation (Mohammad, 2017). Furthermore, an opinion can be expressed explicitly or implicitly (Liu, 2010). For example an opinion regarding the quality of a bag can be expressed explicitly 'The leather of this bag is really good quality' or implicitly 'I've had this bag forever' implying that it is a lasting bag due to its high quality. Also, the same thing can be said in different ways. For example an individual who wants to express a positive sentiment on a dress from Zara could say: 'I love my new Zara dress' or 'I'm in love with Zara's new collection.' In these cases, a machine is likely to detect the positive valence. However, the same sentiment could be expressed with the sentence 'I've never seen anything like this Zara dress.' In this case, manual analysis will be able to identify the positive valence, whereas it could be harder for automatic analysis.

However, reading and manually annotating large sets of data can be a challenging and time-consuming activity. Automatic systems enable to overcome such challenges by being able to analyse vast amounts of data.

Sentiment Research on Social Media

Sentiment analysis is one of the latest developments of text mining, which has gained interest on social media as it is rich in user-generated content. Social media users voluntarily share their opinion and thoughts on the channels, offering a large volume of data, which represents an opportunity for brands to conduct social media monitoring and gain insights on consumers' opinions. Sentiment analysis of data collected from social media provides companies with a high volume of comments, reviews and ratings from users creating opinion-rich resources. This data can be extremely useful in understanding how the business is perceived, opinions and feelings regarding their products or services and insights on how to manage their reputation (Grosse et al., 2015).

Social media data is usually presented in the form of unstructured data. Hence, in order to be analysed, it needs to be structured. The process of finding patterns in unstructured data is called text mining, which involves (i) establishing the corpus of data, (ii) pre-processing it by breaking down the complexity of data and standardising the information and (iii) extracting knowledge to discover patterns. Natural language processing and computational techniques have been developed in order to automatically extract and classify the content in positive or negative. Sentiment extraction approaches can broadly be distinguished in 'bottom up' approaches represented by machine learning and 'top-down,' which are mainly lexicon-based (Jain et al., 2022).

Although social media offers an excellent opportunity for sentiment analysis, it also implies challenges. First, the vast amount of data available on social media channels, even though it represents an opportunity, can be challenging to navigate, monitor and track. Second, individuals' opinions are often part of longer posts; hence, they need to be extracted in order to be analysed. Third, as discussed in other chapters of this book, the content of a social media post can be multimodal. Individuals are increasingly accustomed to expressing their feelings through emojis, in Japanese 'picture character,' a graphic symbol that helps users express feelings, emotions, concepts and ideas in their communications (Kralj Novak et al., 2015). In a short text, such as a tweet or a comment, an emoji can represent an essential piece of information regarding an individual's feeling; thus, it should not be disregarded in the analysis. To facilitate the interpretation of emojis and their positive or negative valence, there are resources for automatic sentiment analysis such as the Emoji Sentiment Ranking developed by Kralj Novak et al. (2015) (http://kt.ijs.si/data/Emoji_sentiment_ranking/index.html). Furthermore, there are websites that monitor the use of emojis, for example emojipedia.org/stats.

Sentiment Analysis in Fashion

Leveraging on big data available on social media, sentiment analysis enables brands to gain insights for marketing intelligence through the analysis of user-generated content.

Sentiment analysis on social media can help fashion brands access real-time information regarding consumers' opinions and respond promptly to their comments. An overview of positive and negative opinions provides the brands the ability to evaluate the strengths and weaknesses of their products and services. Hence, sentiment analysis offers the opportunity to conduct customer satisfaction analysis and thoroughly understand the audience, providing firms with actionable insights through customer feedback on which they can make informed predictions, make decisions, improve customer service and refine product characteristics. It also represents an opportunity to benchmark their strengths and weaknesses against those of competitors. Moreover, sentiment analysis is also effective for crisis management, as monitoring social media can help recognise negative comments and act upon them in a timely manner (Jain et al., 2022; Pantano et al., 2019).

Sentiment Analysis

In order to adequately understand sentiment analysis, it is useful to start from the idea of opinion, which involves various concepts such as sentiment, evaluation and attitude. Sentiment is the positive or negative feeling associated with an entity (product, service, person, issue, organisation) by an opinion holder (Liu, 2010).

Sentiments can be of different types, orientations and intensities.

- *Sentiment types* can be classified as rational (those that do not express any emotion) and emotional (those that imply an emotional sentiment)
- *Sentiment orientation*, also referred to as *polarity*, can be positive, negative or neutral in the case of absence of sentiment. The polarity of words and phrases can be detected manually or through semi-supervised and automatic methods which adopt sentiment resources such as lexicons and datasets: A sentiment lexicon is a labelled repository of words and phrases; sentiment-annotated datasets are labelled documents (Joshi et al., 2017; Mohammad, 2017)
- *Intensity* refers to the strength of the sentiment. Commonly, it is represented with discrete ratings levels, for example, from one to five stars

As previously mentioned, sentiment analysis can be conducted manually or automatically with the support of tools (Mohammad, 2017).

Sentiment analysis utilises natural language processing to extract and interpret opinions from text. It can be conducted at three different levels: Document level, sentence level and feature/aspect level. At the document level, the aim is to identify the overall opinion of the document; at the sentence level, the aim is to identify the sentences that express an opinion and assess its polarity; at the feature level, the aim is to identify the entity and its aspects and then assess the opinion (this level of analysis needs natural language processing).

Two main approaches utilised to automatically conduct sentiment analysis are:

1. Lexicon-based approach
2. Machine learning approach

The lexicon-based approach is an unsupervised learning method that utilises predeveloped dictionaries to calculate the occurrence of positive and negative words.

Each word is given a score, which is then used to assess the sentence valence. For example SentiWordNet is a widely adopted resource for opinion mining.

Machine learning is a supervised learning approach that implies the training of data. A known set of data that has been tagged manually is utilised by the machine to learn which words are positive or negative and then applied to other datasets (Drus and Khalid, 2019).

Steps we suggest to follow while performing a sentiment analysis manually are as follows:

Step 1: Collect the data
Step 2: Clean the data (e.g. remove duplicates, irrelevant sentences and words)
Step 3: Analyse your data:

- Identify the sentiment type (rational or emotional)
- Identify the polarity of the messages (negative, positive or neutral)
- Determine the strength of the sentiment (e.g. from 1 to 5)
- Pay attention to the tone, sarcasm, emojis

Step 4: Get insight from the results and discuss them

Bibliography

Cambria, E., Das, D., Bandyopadhyay, S. and Feraco, A., 2017. *A practical guide to sentiment analysis* (Vol. 5). Springer International Publishing.

Drus, Z. and Khalid, H., 2019. Sentiment analysis in social media and its application: Systematic literature review. *Procedia Computer Science*, *161*, pp. 707–714.

Grosse, K., Gonzalez, M.P., Chesnevar, C.I. and Maguitman, A.G., 2015. Integrating argumentation and sentiment analysis for mining opinions from Twitter. *AI Communications*, *28*(3), pp. 387–401.

Jain, D.K., Boyapati, P., Venkatesh, J. and Prakash, M., 2022. An intelligent cognitive-inspired computing with big data analytics framework for sentiment analysis and classification. *Information Processing & Management*, *59*(1), p. 102758.

Joshi, A., Bhattacharyya, P. and Ahire, S., 2017. Sentiment resources: Lexicons and datasets. In *A practical guide to sentiment analysis* (pp. 85–106). Springer.

Kralj Novak, P., Smailović, J., Sluban, B. and Mozetič, I., 2015. Sentiment of emojis. *PLOS One*, *10*(12), p. e0144296.

Liu, B., 2010. Sentiment analysis and subjectivity. *Handbook of Natural Language Processing*, *2*(2010), pp. 627–666.

Mohammad, S.M., 2017. Challenges in sentiment analysis. In *A practical guide to sentiment analysis* (pp. 61–83). Springer.

Pantano, E., Giglio, S. and Dennis, C., 2019. Making sense of consumers' tweets: Sentiment outcomes for fast fashion retailers through Big Data analytics. *International Journal of Retail & Distribution Management*, *47*(9), pp. 915–927.

Wankhade, M., Rao, A.C.S. and Kulkarni, C., 2022. A survey on sentiment analysis methods, applications, and challenges. *Artificial Intelligence Review*, *55*(7), pp. 5731–5780.

12

ARGUMENTATION ANALYSIS

Introduction

Argumentation originates from rhetoric and philosophy. Rhetoric involves 'the design and realisation of communicative interventions that are persuasive but also well-founded' (Greco and Mazzali-Lurati, 2021, p. 8). The aim of rhetoric is not to be manipulative but to find reason. The importance of reason is highly important in argumentation, as arguers rely on it through the so-called 'topoi-loci,' meaning places—for example 'locus from authority'—from which the arguments are taken in order to back up the claims (Greco and Mazzali-Lurati, 2021, p. 5).

Van Eemeren et al. (2004, p. 1) define argumentation as a 'verbal, social, and rational activity aimed at convincing a reasonable critic of the acceptability of a standpoint by putting forward a constellation of propositions justifying or refuting the proposition expressed in the standpoint.'

Argumentation involves three main elements:

1. A problem, issue or question that generates a difference in opinions
2. A standpoint, the opinion held by one party, which is not accepted by the other party. The standpoint, which is defended by an individual through argumentation, should convince the readers and listeners to accept the argument
3. Reasonable arguments that are used to justify the standpoint

In order for argumentation to take place, there should be a difference in opinions. The differences in opinions can be of various types:

- 'Single and non-mixed opinion' when the standpoint of one party meets doubt from the other party

DOI: 10.4324/9781003505495-17

- 'Mixed opinion' if the other party is doubtful and also has an opposite standpoint
- 'Multiple opinions' if there is more than one proposition

Argumentation includes the arguments and also the broader dialogue in which the arguments take place as an attempt to resolve or avoid disagreement. A proposition can be a description of facts and events, a judgement, a prediction or some advice. Positive, negative or neutral positions can be taken in respect of a proposition. Other modes that are not propositional, such as images, videos, sounds and smells, can be adopted as evidence for a conclusion (multimodal argument). Wider modes of arguing can be useful in the online context, such as social media, where individuals communicate and express their opinions in many different forms (Groarke, 2015).

Argumentation Stages and Structure

According to the pragma-dialectic model, argumentation as a critical discussion aimed at resolving disagreements has four main stages (Van Eemeren, 2016):

1. *The confrontation stage*: The parties establish having a difference of opinion
2. *The opening stage*: The roles of protagonist and antagonist are assigned, and the rules of the discussion are decided
3. *The argumentation stage*: The protagonist defends the standpoint and tries to remove the antagonist doubts
4. *The concluding phase*: The parties decide the extent to which the difference of opinion has been resolved and in whose favour. A difference in opinion can be said to be resolved when one of the two parties revises their initial position.

Although being widely recognised and adopted, other models have been suggested. This idealised model of argumentation that reduces the interaction to that between a protagonist and an antagonist has been challenged by polylogues, which are 'dialogues more complex than simple one-on-one dialogues' (Aakhus and Lewiński, 2017, p. 181). Polylogues potentially involve an infinite number of actors, positions and places. This is especially relevant in the online context, which often involves a variety of users (Greco and De Cock, 2021). The study by Greco and De Cock (2021) shows that in polylogues, an argumentative misalignment in the opening stage could be detrimental to a discussion and lead to a controversy. Specifically, it identifies the misalignment regarding the definition of sustainable fashion as a possible cause of the ongoing controversy surrounding sustainable fashion.

Argumentation can present itself with different structures depending on how the propositions are related to each other:

- *Single argumentation* is formed by one argument
- *Multiple argumentation* consists of more than one defence of the same standpoint

- *Coordinative argumentation* involves the combination of several arguments in defence of a standpoint
- *Subordinative argumentation* consists of arguments supporting arguments

An argument can present flaws. There are two main types of inconsistencies: (i) logical and (ii) pragmatic. A logical inconsistency occurs when statements contradict each other, whereas a pragmatic one occurs when the statements put forward have contradictory consequences in the real world.

Argumentation Research on Social Media

Argumentation research on social media channels offers both opportunities and challenges (Balabanova and Palmieri, 2020; Grosse et al., 2015; Rocci and Pollaroli, 2018; Toni and Torroni, 2011).

In terms of opportunities, social media channels represent a useful source to conduct argumentation analysis as:

- They are widely adopted by users to express their opinions on a variety of topics, resulting in exchanges in the form of discussions between individuals and enabling to explore in-depth individuals' arguments in debates;
- The multimodality nature of social media enables to collect opinions and comments shared in different formats extending the argumentation analysis beyond verbal modes.

Argumentation analysis on social media also presents challenges (Lytos et al., 2019; Schneider et al., 2012).

- Usually 'real' conversations do not always present themselves in a logical structure ready for analysis as many parts of the conversation remain implicit or unexpressed; thus, extracting and reconstructing arguments can prove challenging
- The language utilised on social media, as seen in previous chapters, is often informal presenting the use of slang, abbreviations and emoticons, making the interpretation complicated.

To overcome such challenges, research has focused on computational linguistics in order to automatically extract arguments from social networks (Grosse et al., 2015).

Argumentation Analysis in Fashion

Telling compelling stories is extremely important. The stories must be interesting, persuasive and should be able to attract consumers' attention. Storytelling should also enable brands to build customer relationships and develop trust. To do so, the stories told have to be credible as consumers are increasingly empowered by having access to various sources of information. Argumentation analysis represents a method to analyse multimodal social media content with a critical outlook. It enables to retrieve what is the standpoint brought forward by the speaker, which arguments are adopted to support it and, finally, how to evaluate their soundness.

It also represents a useful method to study relevant debates and discover different sides to an argument (Jones, 2020). Furthermore, it enables us to analyse not only the argument of the firms' official communication but also the arguments by other parties such as activists, influencers, fashion curators and UGC, trying to persuade through reasonable arguments (Greco, 2023).

For example Greco et al. (2021) and Greco and De Cock (2021) show how argumentation analysis on social media can be useful to analyse the controversy of fashion sustainability.

Argumentation Analysis

In order to conduct argumentation analysis, it is necessary to reconstruct the way in which one tries to convince the audience regarding the acceptability of the standpoint put forward. The process of reconstruction can involve (i) deletion, (ii) addition, (iii) permutation and (iv) substitution (Van Eemeren and Houtlosser, 2003).

i. Deletion: The elimination of elements that are not relevant for the analysis
ii. Addition: The integration of implicit and indirect elements that are needed but left unexpressed in the discourse
iii. Permutation: Ordering and rearranging elements to reconstruct the discourse by putting the standpoint first and then the arguments
iv. Substitution: Reformulating unclear and ambiguous expressions

In order to analyse the acts of arguing and the arguments, it is necessary to identify the premises and conclusions, referred to as 'dressing' the argument (Groarke, 2015, p. 135). In some cases, it is easy and obvious to identify them, whereas in other more complex cases, it is necessary to identify and decide how to manage degressions, rewordings, implicit premises and conclusions, rhetorical questions and vague claims (Groarke, 2015).

Caution should be taken in identifying the standpoint. Sometimes, it is possible to identify it by searching for indicators such as 'because,' 'since'. . . (retrogressive as the standpoint precedes the argument) or 'thus,' 'therefore'. . . (progressive as the standpoint follows). Yet, caution should be taken as these indicators could be misleading; for example 'because' could be used to introduce causes rather than reasons (Van Eemeren et al., 2002).

The following steps are proposed on the basis of the study by Balabanova and Palmieri (2020):

Step 1: Define the research question(s) to be answered
Step 2: Dataset: Collect the posts according to study criteria on the relevant platform(s)

- Timeframe
- Language
- Hashtags, keywords

Step 3: Analyse the data (text or multimodal): Read and code the data following a coding scheme:

- Identify the standpoints of the actors: What argument does the brand use to support its position?
  Positions: For example does the post have a supportive (advocate), attacking (criticism) or neutral position towards the issue?
  Is the argument sound? (check for inconsistencies)
- Argumentativeness: How are justifications for or against the claims expressed in the post?
  - 'Justified opinion': Posts with both a claim and at least one argument for this claim
  - 'Opinion': Posts without an explicit argument
  - 'Refutation': Posts in which an argument is made against an opposite claim
  - 'No opinion': Posts that do not contain any claims (Balabanova and Palmieri, 2020)

Example of Argumentation Analysis from a Fashion Study

An example of an academic study that has adopted argumentation analysis is presented in order to give an overview of the steps followed to collect and analyse the data.

The study titled 'Victims or agents for change? Representations and self-representations of women in the social media debate surrounding sustainable fashion' by Greco et al. (2021) adopts argumentation analysis to study how women are represented and self-represented in the social media debate surrounding sustainable fashion.

Step 1: Research question: How are women discursively represented and self-represented in the social media debate surrounding sustainable fashion?
Step 2: Dataset

- Channels: Instagram and Twitter

- Timeframe: Posts published during April 20–26, 2020 (Fashion Revolution Week)
- Language: English, Spanish, Portuguese, Italian, French, German, Dutch
- Hashtag: #fashionrevolution
- Keywords: Words related to women in seven languages
- Final dataset: Seven tweets and 278 Instagram posts (after having eliminated commercial posts with no argumentative content)

Step 3: Analysis
Coding scheme—code occurrences according to the following categories:

- The category of a woman (e.g. garment workers)
- General mention of the category of women or specific examples (e.g. providing the name of a woman working at a specific brand), representation or self-representation
- Agentivity
- Stock issues

Results

- Identification of two main message categories: (i) The ill—those that highlight the presence of a problem and (ii) the cure—those that also suggest a solution to the problem.
- Generally, women are presented as agents who play an active role in contributing to the solution and never as the cause of the issue.

Bibliography

Aakhus, M. and Lewiński, M., 2017. Advancing polylogical analysis of large-scale argumentation: Disagreement management in the fracking controversy. *Argumentation, 31*, pp. 179–207.

Balabanova, E. and Palmieri, R., 2020. *Talking at cross-purpose? ASOS, Twitter and the fast-fashion backlash.* Report (pp. 1–24). Figshare.

Greco, S., 2023. Twitter activists' argumentation through subdiscussions: Theory, method and illustration of the controversy surrounding sustainable fashion. *Argumentation, 37*(1), pp. 1–23.

Greco, S. and De Cock, B., 2021. Argumentative misalignments in the controversy surrounding fashion sustainability. *Journal of Pragmatics, 174*, pp. 55–67.

Greco, S. and Mazzali-Lurati, S., 2021. Rhetoric. In *The Palgrave encyclopedia of the possible*. Palgrave Macmillan. https://doi.org/10.1007/978-3-319-98390-5_8-3.

Greco, S., Mercuri, C. and De Cock, B., 2021. Victims or agents for change? Representations and self-representations of women in the social media debate surrounding sustainable fashion. *Babylonia, 3*, p. 90.

Groarke, L., 2015. Going multimodal: What is a mode of arguing and why does it matter? *Argumentation, 29*, pp. 133–155.

Grosse, K., Gonzalez, M.P., Chesnevar, C.I. and Maguitman, A.G., 2015. Integrating argumentation and sentiment analysis for mining opinions from Twitter. *AI Communications, 28*(3), pp. 387–401.

Jones, K.B., 2020. American Vogue and sustainable fashion (1990–2015): A multimodal critical discourse analysis. *Clothing and Textiles Research Journal*, *38*(2), pp. 104–118.

Lytos, A., Lagkas, T., Sarigiannidis, P. and Bontcheva, K., 2019. The evolution of argumentation mining: From models to social media and emerging tools. *Information Processing & Management*, *56*(6), p. 102055.

Rocci, A. and Pollaroli, C., 2018. Introduction: Multimodality in argumentation. *Semiotica*, *2018*(220), pp. 1–17.

Schneider, J., Davis, B. and Wyner, A., 2012. Dimensions of argumentation in social media. In *International conference on knowledge engineering and knowledge management* (pp. 21–25). Springer.

Toni, F. and Torroni, P., 2011. Bottom-up argumentation. In *International workshop on theorie and applications of formal argumentation* (pp. 249–262). Springer.

Van Eemeren, F.H., 2016. Identifying argumentative patterns: A vital step in the development of pragma-dialectics. *Argumentation*, *30*(1), pp. 1–23.

Van Eemeren, F.H., Grootendorst, R. and Grootendorst, R., 2004. *A systematic theory of argumentation: The pragma-dialectical approach*. Cambridge University Press.

Van Eemeren, F.H., Grootendorst, R. and Henkemans, A.F.S., 2002. *Argumentation: Analysis, evaluation, presentation*. Routledge.

Van Eemeren, F.H. and Houtlosser, P., 2003. The development of the pragma-dialectical approach to argumentation. *Argumentation*, *17*, pp. 387–403.

SECTION 5
Interviews with Fashion Brands

Introduction

The aim of this section is to provide insights into the social media practices of fashion brands through the interviews conducted with the representatives of selected fashion brands.

The interviewees discuss the ways in which social media is managed by the brands, including the brand's social media presence, strategy and design, relationship with other stakeholders and the way in which the social media performance is measured. Furthermore, the challenges of managing social media and future outlooks are discussed.

Through the interviews, the main theoretical concepts presented in this book are discussed with industry professionals.

The first interview was conducted in Switzerland with Nicolas Girotto, CEO of Bally. Bally is a Swiss luxury fashion house founded by Carl Franz Bally in 1851. It is among one of the oldest European luxury brands. Bally is known for its heritage and craftsmanship. It offers bags, accessories and ready-to-wear collection. The interview with the CEO of the brand addresses the strategic overview of the social media importance for branding and community engagement.

The second interview was done with the representative of another Spanish brand—Cortefiel (part of the TENDAM Group). Cortefiel was created in 1945, and today is one of the most well-known Spanish fashion retailers abroad. The conversation with Blanca Rosa del Bosque, responsible for Digital and Media relations of the brand, opened up several internal practices and daily activities of the social media management within a fashion brand.

The interviews took place in October and November 2022 and were conducted by the authors of this book.

DOI: 10.4324/9781003505495-18

13

INTERVIEW WITH NICOLAS GIROTTO, CEO OF BALLY

What is social media for Bally?

Social media is one of the platforms to discuss and reach our audience. It is an integral part of our marketing mix, and we see it as a way to engage with our community, to communicate our brand. It is really an element of branding more than conversion.

If you want to discover a brand these days, it comes naturally for most of us to go through social media and to look at the brand—it is the first source of information. Sometimes there might be some confusion on whether social media is utilised for conversion or branding. For Bally, social media is a branding and community engagement tool.

Who is in charge of Bally's social media and who is taking the decisions?

Multiple persons are responsible for social media because now it is so large that you don't really have one person in charge of social media in the company.

Social media covers different aspects—I previously mentioned branding and content—so you have to think about the content to post from the beginning. It is not about producing content for other media and then trying to adapt it to social media. Instead, it is about thinking from the very beginning about the content in these different formats. For this reason, we have a team specialising in social media.

Then, in the marketing team, we have people who are pushing this content. They are trying to reach an audience; they think about who we want to target and how to get the best return on advertising spend.

Now it is important to have digital experts who have a qualified point of view on all aspects of social media. So, I'm saying that on one side, it touches multiple departments, and on the other side, it is important that there is one person who has a qualified opinion. For this reason, I have appointed a chief digital officer who has

DOI: 10.4324/9781003505495-19

expertise in digital marketing, communication and a more technical background. She works closely with the social media team to make sure that social media campaigns are successful. So, for the latest show that we did (Fall/Winter 2022), the digital component was very important to maximise visibility. For example, the show was live-streamed on YouTube and our own website.

How are social media channels connected to the marketing objectives of the brand?

Social media is an integral part; we do not make any distinction now. If we look at our marketing mix, for example if we take 100 CHF being spent on promoting the brand—how much do we spend on social media? It is a very important part, definitely a double-digit percentage. There is no question on whether we invest in social media or not, and we cannot think of one campaign where there is no presence on social media.

Social media allows us to communicate directly with our customers and receive feedback from our audience; these are key benefits that we see from investing in social media.

How does Bally design the social media strategy?

The way in which we design a campaign on social media is really in function of who we want to reach. We ask ourselves: What are the objectives of the campaign? If you want to launch a new product and reach a younger clientele you will not use the same social media as when you want to push and promote some of your iconic products: In the first case we will use channels such as TikTok while in the second one we will use more traditional channels such as Instagram.

So, it really depends on who you want to reach and also on the region in which you would like to be present. A large part of our clientele is in Asia; their habits and their social media use are completely different to those of Western customers. For this reason, we have a localised team that masters social media in different regions and can provide advice on the content that would work best in different countries.

How do you manage the relationships with other members in the social media ecosystem of Bally?

We have an internal team that is dedicated to community engagement.

In terms of relationships, we strongly believe in 'good sense.' Obviously, we have some social media policies we need to adhere to on our personal social media accounts. For example if in the show-room there are new products that are not on the market yet, Bally's employees should not post about them on their personal social media channels.

Could you say a few words on how Bally measures their social media presence and performance?

With social media, it is more a question of whether the KPIs are really relevant. It seems to be the magic of social media that you can really measure everything, but the challenge is to be sure that the KPIs used represent something that truly reflects your performance. With print, it was harder to measure the effectiveness of a campaign as the data available was limited. Now, with social media, you have tons of data, and you can really track the effectiveness and the returns of your campaign. The challenge is the effectiveness of these measures and if they reflect reality. So, measuring ROI on social media is very easy as you have many KPIs, but at the same time, it is very challenging.

If and how is Bally's approach to social media changing?

There are a lot of changes in social media: you need to evolve and be fast in capturing the latest trends and building the community. If you are late, the cost is very high. Right now, if you want to grow your space on Instagram, it is very expensive because it is a very mature platform, so the cost of acquiring followers is very high. This is why I was mentioning the hiring of the digital chief officer, to have a person who is fully immersed in social media and who is able to make the right decisions at an early stage—What is the platform that is only a marketing gimmick that will die in six months? What is the platform that we should invest in? It is about making the right choices. For example we had a lot of debates in China—should we invest in WeChat and Weibo?

Also, understanding the model of each platform is essential. Little Red Book was difficult to understand when the team was promoting to invest in it. There is a need to adapt; there is a need to understand. We realise that this is a kind of constant disruption; going back to my previous point, it is important to have a qualified team.

What were the motivations behind erasing all the content to start fresh? Why would a brand like Bally adopt such a strategy?

It was a difficult decision for the brand to archive all our posts—they are not cancelled—in order to show a new version of ourselves without forgetting who we are. We wanted to show a new version of ourselves in a consistent way.

Brand discovery often happens on social media so looking at the feed is important to give a good representation of who the brand is, so archiving the posts from the past was a decision that allowed us to give a representation of ourselves that is more consistent and also a kind of marketing stunt. With the new marketing director, you are erasing everything to tease a bit. You want to show through an element of change and disruption, so there are multiple objectives. It is not an easy decision as you do not want to be disrespectful to the past and the customers who have been loving what we have been doing in the past.

How do you believe social media will evolve and develop?

As a CEO, I am not an expert on social media and I want to be very humble, but what we see right now is social media channels that are becoming more and more genuine, where it is not about the perfect version of yourself and of the brand. It is something that should be telling the true story of who you are as a person and as a brand.

So, this is impacting the brands and how we communicate; we have been producing for certain platforms content that is much more behind the scenes in order to be genuine. For the latest show (Fall/Winter 2022), we had different kinds of content for different platforms, and this authenticity was important in order to engage with our audience and make them feel part of the show.

I feel that the attention will change; it will decrease. I see an increase in awareness about how much time we spend on social media channels. This will also be reflected in how we should communicate and engage with our audience and also the time we should dedicate to social media. This can also be a question for the brand and how you are investing in social media; as we are investing money in these channels we want to be seen, but we need to find the right balance.

What would you say the benefits of social media can be for a luxury brand such as Bally?

The benefits are reaching an audience, a qualified audience, because you can segment much more whom you will reach. You do not really control or know who will open a magazine, instead, with social media you can know who is looking at your posts, your reels and live streams. So, I think segmentation is really one of the best features of it.

Social media are also quite seamless, you can react fairly quickly and be sure of the message that you are sending.

What about the critical issues in managing social media for a fashion brand?

Social media challenges are definitely with the returns you might have or not have.

We are investing more and more money in social media, and sometimes you can say to yourself it is starting to be a lot of money, maybe I should be investing more in prints. It is about comparing the different channels. On social media you have the feeling of being in control of what you are doing and measuring everything, but it is difficult to measure the effectiveness versus other forms of media because when you are opening a beautiful magazine, you know that it is staying on the coffee table for a long time and that it will contribute differently to the brand's equity.

So, social media effectiveness can be questioned compared to other media. For example we measure impressions and engagement, but we could question whether the content really sticks with the audience. Is it actually good for the brand?

14

INTERVIEW WITH BLANCA ROSA DEL BOSQUE MADERA, DIGITAL & MEDIA MANAGER, TENDAM FASHION GROUP

What is social media for your brand?

Social media is the biggest 'shop window' for our brand. It is the place where we need to show our best side. In our particular case, it also acts as an important channel to draw in new and younger customers that we can later dress, when they are in a more mature phase in terms of fashion. With our core target belonging to Generation X and also reaching Baby Boomers, it's difficult to get through to this target audience through social media. In other words, we work now for future engagement. In the last few years, thanks to the inclusion of the e-commerce product feed in social media accounts, we have identified that it's a good way to generate traffic and sales.

Who is in charge of social media, and who makes the decisions?

Some years ago, we had a digital manager on the marketing team who was in charge of social media. However, this role naturally disappeared owing to the fact that every profile in the marketing department eventually developed and was expected to have a digital vision. Since then, the content manager has been responsible for social media and usually works with social media agencies and content creators specialising in fashion.

How is social media connected to the marketing objectives of the brand?

We work in social media in different stages of the conversion funnel, and we use them for both the awareness phase and the consideration and purchase phases, creating different content or paid media strategies depending on the goals; but, overall, we use them to generate both brand and 'top-of-mind' awareness.

DOI: 10.4324/9781003505495-20

How do you design the social media strategy?
In our case, social media does not depend on the promotional strategy as much as email marketing or in-store communication does. However, there are social trends that we follow:

Before we get down to work on the strategy, we analyse what the competitors are doing and what results they have through several social analytics services. We then start designing the strategy by defining the brand pillars; in our case, there are three: fashion, sustainability and innovation. We create content (photos or videos) to communicate these attributes, always posting in accordance with product availability. It is a very meticulous work that can be scuppered if there are delays in the arrival of the merchandise, as that requires changing the whole content calendar.

On which platforms is Cortefiel active, and for what reasons?
Nowadays, our most important social activity happens on Instagram. We also upload some content on Facebook because, as I mentioned, our core customers are mature (45+ years), and they still use this platform despite the fact that it is losing power year after year.

Pinterest has been a great discovery for us; after launching a test, we found the results to be very satisfactory in terms of engagement and traffic to the online store. Therefore, we currently try to upload new content on a weekly basis. I feel the products look very attractive on this platform because of the innovative interface design—they were one of the first to have a functionality that recommended similar product images instantaneously upon searching.

TikTok is the next social network that we ought to tackle; however, with 40% of its users aged between 16 and 24, we still have some time to work on the strategy for this platform before the mature public arrives. The communication codes are very different on TikTok, so the challenge will be to find our tone and style.

How do you manage the relationships with other members of the social media ecosystem?
When we work on the social strategy and define the messages we want to launch in the market, we decide who the best ambassador to spread the word will be. We think about all the aforementioned roles. All of them are essential, and, personally, I'm a big supporter of the user-generated content and micro-influencers. This kind of content sometimes works better than that created by top influencers because it looks more real: the 'models' could be you, and the clothes could look just as good on you as they do on them.

Creative directors and stylists also star in some campaigns, such as those that present special or limited collections. Employees are, after all, the best prescribers for social and corporate responsibility activity.

Could you say a few words on how your brand measures its social media presence and performance?
We have access to different social analytic platforms. On a weekly basis, we analyse fan growth as well as the best and worst content in terms of reach and engagement. In terms of measuring users' intention to buy, we also look at how much traffic is driven to the online store via social media. This information is then analysed every month and each semester—always comparing results against those of our competitors. Social networks also have their own dashboards, which are a useful way to access certain data quickly; that said, I would recommend putting together a social hub that collects data from every network—including that of competitors—in order to analyse it more thoroughly.

Is your Brand approach to social media changing? If it is, how is it changing?
Until a year ago, our social media profiles were focused on promoting only one brand: Cortefiel. After the acquisition of new brands such as Slowlove or Hoss Intropia and creating OOTO (our new brand for men), we made a decision to sell these brands at Cortefiel stores to attract new target audiences while offering a wide range of products to our current customers. Subsequently, we asked ourselves, 'What would happen if we posted about SlowLove and Hoss Intropia products on the Cortefiel social profiles?' This led us to ask, 'Should the Cortefiel profile post about the Cortefiel brand only, or should we promote the new Cortefiel multi-brand concept?' In the end, we took a bet on the multi-brand concept, and the latest numbers show that the decision is being well-received. This allows us to create a higher quantity of looks, thereby offering a larger variety of content (in fact, sometimes there is more content than we are able to publish), and, of course, this is fantastic because we can simply choose the best!

How do you believe social media will evolve and develop?
It's hard to say, but my feeling is that real content has the best performance: the more natural you are, the better results you get. I think the future will revolve around real people.

In terms of format, it's been increasingly difficult to achieve real engagement over the last few years, and the challenge is to create something memorable that lasts no more than 15 seconds. This requires being very creative and direct. Content that involves music and dancing is doing well . . . people want to have fun. Other content that is proving to be successful is tutorial videos. In fashion this could mean *how to dress for a formal party, how to organise your wardrobe, how to create two looks with the same blazer*. . . this kind of thing never goes out of fashion.

What would you say the benefits of social media can be for your brand?
Social media allows people to get to know brands better and talk to them face-to-face, creating a dialogue between brands and consumers. As a brand, you can get direct feedback from your customers by, for example, launching a 24-hour survey that tests a new brand ambassador. This is extremely valuable because it allows you to make quick decisions that optimise your marketing budget in a matter of days.

What about the critical success factors?
Never disappointed and always listening to your audience is key to being successful in social networks. Everything you have created over the years can suddenly be lost because of one bad decision.

We recently encountered a situation that resulted in high tension: a campaign quickly became controversial among our community due to our choice of ambassador. The way we reacted emerged to be crucial going forward. We decided to separate the comments into those coming from haters and those being expressed by real customers who were generously giving their sincere opinions. We ignored the former but listened to the latter by writing personalised direct messages to all of them individually. We placed the power in their hands by asking them to choose the next face of the brand. As a result, we strengthened our relationship with these followers, who were both surprised and grateful as we listened to their opinions.

Made in the USA
Monee, IL
17 June 2025

0483fa3a-5c78-4bd4-8e3b-a8adfae1f4f3R01